M-Mème

An Idea to Eliminate Conflict

Dr. Prasad Mallipudi

This is a work of nonfiction. The events and the incidents mentioned in the book are true and real. However, some names and characteristics have been changed, some events have been compressed, and some dialogues have been recreated.

First Edition: October 2025
Printed in India

Printed at: Gapmeta Ventures Pvt. Ltd., Navi Mumbai
Typeset in Adobe Garamond Pro
ISBN: 978-93-6070-101-7

Cover Design: Prajakta Sawant

STORYMIRROR
Stories that reflect you

Publisher: StoryMirror Infotech Pvt. Ltd.
Unit No-F/705, 7th Floor, Kailas Corporate Lounge,
Veer Savarkar Road, Vikhroli Park Site,
Vikhroli West, Mumbai-400079,
Maharashtra, India.

Web: storymirror.com
Facebook: @storymirror
Twitter: @story_mirror
Instagram: @storymirror
Email: marketing@storymirror.com

Book Website: m-meme.in
Email: info@m-meme.in

Dedicated to Humanity

ACKNOWLEDGEMENTS

Author offers respectful salutations to his parents, Smt. Jagadamba and Sri Venkata Rao and all his teachers, starting with Sri Somayajulu, who taught him the alphabet. According to Indian spiritual tradition, the prayers start with Sri Ganesha followed by Lord Shiva (or Lord Krishna), the all-pervading Consciousness, as *Adi Guru* - first teacher.

And then there is the *Guru Parampara* - succession of teachers, leading to many lineages. We all are indebted to many people through whom we received the knowledge and spiritual tools. The author bows down to Sri Sankara, Sri Ramana, Sri Nisargadatta, Sri Yellamraju Srinivasa Rao, all the prophets, seers and saints of all religions and scientists who have shared their wisdom for the betterment of humankind.

The author is indebted to Dr. R. Srinivasa Reddy for guiding in the spiritual journey, helping with the manuscript and writing the foreword. The author is grateful to Sri Harshavardhan Madabhushi for going through the manuscript and writing the foreword.

Profound thanks to Bibhu, Sneha, Prajakta and all the good people at StoryMirror for their help in the publishing process. Thanks to many people at various companies, especially at Adobe, Airtel, Amazon, Dell, Google, Microsoft and Whatsapp, who made the process of writing this book easy.

Having come from a family of farmers, the author thanks farmers all over the world, the people in the food processing and food supply chains, who are providing us with daily sustenance.

Finally, a big thank you to Kamala, Vishnu, Pranav, family, friends, colleagues, students, staff, patients, readers, and all acquaintances for being a part of the author's life and helping him along in his life journey as well as the spiritual path.

FOREWORD

Every so often, a book comes along that doesn't just inform; it resonates. It does not merely challenge our thinking; it stirs something deeper within us, something ancient yet often forgotten. M-Mème is one such rare work.

This book is born not of theory, but of lived experience, of a mind that has questioned deeply, a heart that has searched sincerely, and a soul that refuses to settle for partial truths. In these pages, the author does not prescribe a single path but rather invites us to examine the many - religion, science, philosophy, and ultimately, the path within. With clarity and courage, he explores the tensions and illusions that divide us, while gently pointing towards the indivisible truth that unites all of existence.

Reading M-Mème is not like reading a typical spiritual text. It feels like sitting down with a trusted companion who has walked through confusion, disillusionment, faith, and insight; and who now shares what he has found, not with authority, but with humility.

This is a book for those who have achieved much in the world yet feel something essential remains unfulfilled. It is for those who are weary of conflict; within themselves, between faiths, and across societies. And it is for those who, like the author, have come to realize that lasting peace must begin with clarity in one's own mind.

The author reminds us that true spirituality transcends language, culture, and religion. It is not about conversion, but about convergence: where science and scriptures, East and West, form and formless, all meet in the stillness of Awareness.

As a fellow seeker, I am grateful for this work. This book is both a mirror and a map. May it guide you inward, upward, and beyond.

Dr. R. Srinivasa Reddy
Columbia, South Carolina

FOREWORD

When I began reading the chapter "Division and Union", which was initially shared with me by the author to elicit my comments, I was pleasantly surprised and equally taken aback, as the author is well aware of my vacillation towards agnosticism. My first reaction upon reading the chapter was that this briefest attempt at the boundless literature on spirituality which is being bundled into a concise version would inevitably camouflage the intent of spirituality. As a person who has a fair amount of understanding about spirituality, I thought condensing the subject to the point of stifling would be subjecting it to suffocation. But later, when I read the entire treasure of his treatise on spirituality, I realized that the first one was just a teaser released to me. The herculean effort that was embarked upon by the author was in fact written and rewritten by innumerable seers in volumes the world over from the period of antiquity. Despite it, what is astounding is that the author demonstrated his courage of conviction to focus on the given subject with his incisive intellectual luminosity all along.

The purity of flow of thought in the book is as pristine and as divine as the flow of the River Ganges straight from its origin at Gangothri. The ease and aplomb with which the author laboured his articulation to put across his ideas to the reader is a sheer euphony that creates a joyful jugglery of consonance with the harmony of words, to enable the rendering to be a lilting song in the ears of the reader which unfolds a mellifluous musical concert of spirituality.

With the author's ocean of abundant knowledge coupled with his genial writing skills, and with his catholicity of outlook on life and wisdom which is devoid of a doctrinaire approach to traditional narrow sectarian religious conservatism that we come across very often nowadays, I have no doubt whatsoever that this book would inevitably help unravel not only the separations within the unfathomable depths of the individual mind but also the deep divisions existing in humankind causing chaos in an otherwise hospitable Mother Nature. The author's indefatigable industry will surely be a beacon, the lighthouse of spirituality in the minds of people who are going through the rigmarole of mundane drudgery and monotony of life cycles. For thinking brains, it shall be an elixir of inexplicably enriching and rewarding experience. At the very least, the reader can taste the nectar of spirituality from a whole new perspective and dimension.

Harshavardhan Madabhushi
Hyderabad

PROLOGUE

The author, a practicing surgeon in the south Indian city of Hyderabad, was born into a well-to-do family and was a high achiever in early life. As is a common experience, with every achievement, he would experience a high state of happiness. Over time he realized that the happiness was short-lived, the mind wanted further achievement and was always restless. This made him disenchanted with materialistic achievements and began to have thoughts like, "Is there more to this life?", "What is the purpose of this life?" and "Who am I?" Science and psychology might call this midlife crisis or burning out. This turned the author towards spirituality or metaphysics. As you know there is a wealth of information in the form of scriptures belonging to different religions, and various interpretations and differences within the same religion.

It is the author's firm conviction that the Truth cannot be multiple. It is this point the author wants to emphasize, which forms the crux of this book, for you to remember and hold on firmly. Don't just be a pawn in the material-political-religious-spiritual maze. Try to understand true spirituality, true purpose of religion and the scriptures, and understand your true self. Approach the issue with keen interest; an open, rational and analytical mind. The knowledge the author has acquired and the experiences that he had are the basis of this book. It will be of use to all; and more so to anyone who wants to know more about various aspects of metaphysics or spirituality.

Everyone must do this exercise at some point in life. Do not believe in anyone's narrative. Dive deep into the religious teachings of whatever religion you are following and other religions, get to the bottom of things and try to find the true meaning and purpose of those teachings, which will lead to the ultimate Truth. The author shares the view of Sri Satyanarayana Goenka and Sri Jiddu Krishnamurti, in that you should be your own master. Find out the Truth for yourself first and then you can pass on your first-hand information to the next generation. Otherwise, the Truth remains elusive. Blind faith and dogma based on God, religion, and various other things, including science, will continue to divide the human psyche at individual and collective (society) levels.

One particular group of people the author recommends this book and exploring spirituality to is the people over the age of 60, who have retired from active work and/or financially secure. Even though they have fulfilled their responsibilities well and are financially stable, some restlessness haunts them. It is not so obvious when one is involved in some active work and is young. As one is advancing in age, this becomes more troublesome. The restlessness is due to the partition in one's mind which is innate. The partition and the consequent restlessness can be overcome by proper spiritual quest, knowledge, and contemplation.

Prasad Mallipudi
Sringeri, May 2025

CONTENTS

INTRODUCTION

The purpose of this book is to try to give an overarching view about the nature of life, God, spirituality and related aspects, unravel some of the misconceptions held in society and to nudge people towards proper spirituality which transcends religion and dualities in the mind, and reduces conflict.

As mentioned in the prologue, there is a bewildering array of religions, sub-sects within the same religion, teachings and practices, all of which can be considered as "concepts". There are a variety of concepts existing in the world, everyone thinking and claiming that their religion (or spiritual group) and their concepts are better than the rest, if not the only truth. There is conflict between various religions, their concepts and scientific proof. Along the line it occurred to the author that whatever all the religions or science may be saying, whatever our beliefs may be, the Truth must be one only. Slowly he started realizing that there is a commonality in all the original religious teachings, some of it congruent with modern scientific observations.

Just to give a few examples: There is a hymn praising the feminine goddess Sri Lalitha with a thousand names. Some of the initial names happen to be a vivid description of the "Big bang" that astrophysicists propose is the beginning of the universe. The great Sanskrit poet Sri Kalidasa wrote "*Vaagarthaviva sampruktau*" which is a powerful statement about the fundamental nature of creation, where the act of speaking and the meanings conveyed are inextricably linked in bringing the universe into being (Raghuvamsa 1:1). This sits fair and squarely with: In the beginning was the Word, and the Word was with God, and the Word was God. (John 1:1). The attributes of Allah match quite closely to that of Nirguna Brahman of the Upanishads. If you leave aside the language used, names and forms, the essence is the same.

The core spiritual teachings of the major religions originated thousands of years ago. There are some controversies about the exact time period of different scriptures, but one should not let that divert the mind. The main reason for the diversity is that the scriptures were given by various seers in different time zones and geographic locations in different languages, based on their own understanding and realization of Truth and the need of the society at that particular period and location. Subsequently these teachings were organized into various religions and sub-sects. The wealth of scriptures is from the Indian sub-continent. All the spiritual teachings come in a rather cryptic way, making it difficult for most people to understand and more importantly allowing for misinterpretation.

It is important for us to realize that the seers meant their teachings for all humanity, not just a group of people. Definitely not to use them to fight with each other. The author tried to keep things as simple as possible. If you like all or any of the things in this book, you can implement them to better your life. If you do not like it, simply hit the delete button and forget about it, partly or in whole. The reason for saying this is: not to allow your mind to get confused with new ideas or concepts and start dissecting yet again. As we will see in the later part of the book, the mind plays a divisive game all the time.

If you look deeply, you will find some sort of restlessness, insecurity, fear or some void. This may not be apparent when you are young, but as age increases, if you are honest with yourself, you will notice it. It may take any form; fear of losing something, fear of failure, fear of ill health, fear of death, something or the other. This is due to the division created by the mind that you as a physical entity are separate from the rest of the universe. People resort to several things from acquiring materialistic things to various religious rituals to get over this sense of a void. The restlessness will not go away until the division created by the mind is understood and overcome.

There are some people who are so engrossed in life that they keep going about life without any thoughts of what life is and what the purpose of this life is. If you are happy doing what you are doing and want to continue to live that way, this book is not for you. You may still like to see the simple things to follow in life towards the end of this book. This book is for people who are not happy in life for whatever reason and who want to overcome their negative feelings, especially fear, anger, restlessness and sense of void. It is also for people who are successful in the materialistic life but want to explore beyond the mundane life.

What the author is sharing is age-old wisdom from various spiritual paths, mostly the wisdom from Indian subcontinent. Please do not think that the author is selling Hinduism through the back door. As you will come to see later in this book, the real Truth is beyond all concepts and "isms" which are human made. Truth is beyond them. The concepts are very useful on the spiritual path and some like "self-restraint" are even mandatory, but one must eventually transcend and go beyond all "isms" and concepts to realize the ultimate Truth. Think of them as a scaffold to reach the peak of a summit. Once you reach the summit, you should not cling to the scaffold. You should have reverence for the scaffold but not cling to it. Otherwise, you will not enjoy the beauty at the summit. As one is going up the mountain, the view changes and one feels he/

she can see better than those on the ground, which is true. As one climbs further, the view becomes even better. However, one cannot see what is happening on the other side of the mountain. People and seers of different religions have climbed the mountain from different sides using different methods and are giving their view of things. Only someone who reaches the summit can see all the paths and wholeness. Stick to your path until you reach the summit. Any Self-realized or God-realized (both are the same) person automatically becomes secular.

The title is borrowed from physics and evolutionary theories. M-theory is a theory in physics that unifies all consistent versions of superstring theory. (Superstring theory is an attempt to explain all of the particles and fundamental forces of nature in one theory by modelling them as vibrations of tiny supersymmetric strings - Wikipedia.) M-theory is a theory that tries to encompass all the theories in physics because no single theory can explain all the observed phenomena in the universe. "M-Concept" might have been a good title, because this book encompasses most of the religious paths and spiritual teachings.

Then the "Mème" from the book "The Selfish Gene" came along. It can be translated as an idea that propagates itself from brain to brain through generations. It is pronounced as in "crème". It is perhaps a bit cheeky in taking the name from two scientists who tried to prove there is no God.

As far as the author can envision, science and our ancient scriptures point to the same phenomenon. Science looks at only the observable phenomenon, whereas spirituality looks beyond to the unmanifest creative force behind the manifest observable phenomenon. It is the hope of the author that this all-encompassing concept will propagate itself through the minds of people and reduce conflict.

The intention in sharing these thoughts is to lessen the human misery and the collective destruction we are causing to our home, planet Earth, in pursuit of material comforts and superficial happiness. Once a person understands oneself, the divisive nature of one's mind, and tries to lessen the conflicts (restlessness) in one's own mind, the collective conflict in society will also go down.

Our lives are intricately related to nature. If you try to move away from nature by artificial means, you get emptier and dissatisfied. You must look into yourself to complete the circle of evolution. Psychologically, emotionally, one must travel back, all the way back to single-celled organism (some of you may know that our life starts as a single cell in a mother's womb), primeval soup, big bang where time breaks down and one attains timelessness and deathlessness. Sounds daunting, but possible. Even if one cannot go all the way, just understanding the principle and making some effort will change the life of the individual as well as the collective.

The word God is used many times in this book. Some people may be averse to that word. It is synonymous with "Creator", "Nature", "Cosmic Energy", "Unmanifest", "Being", "Transcendental Reality", "Supreme Being", "Truth", "Ultimate", "Mother Supreme", "Holy Father", "Allah", or anything of one's choice.

Who named God? It is the human mind. The all-pervasive energy or consciousness is present long before the existence of human species. Check the Nasadiya Sukta (Rigveda 10:129), which explores the profound existential and cosmological questions about the origins of the universe and the limits of human knowledge. It is the seers who gave names to various things and tried to explain the process of creation with the available vocabulary and means of communication. The Source of this creation is the same, whatever name may be given to that entity. There is no name or form to that Source. Who can name That which existed before the creation itself? "That" is a nameless, formless, genderless entity beyond any description. It existed long before the human race. Names came much later.

Each of the topics or concepts covered in this book are big topics in themselves. Volumes have been written in the past by various people with different levels of understanding. It is not possible to do justice to each of the topics in this small book. Please read further based on your interest. Author has provided some of the sources that he had studied. You can explore for yourself the vast information on the net. One word of caution: do not be baffled by different explanations. Reconcile the differences and look for commonality. If you keep wondering who is correct, you may not progress. Author's technique is to hang on to the common principle in the information available and move forward. The goal is not to get stuck. Anything that is not congruent is kept aside, not discarded. It may fall into place after some time with more information or better understanding.

Author has taken some verses from the Holy Bible. It is just that the author is familiar with Christianity due to his stay in the UK for some time. Many of you may be aware that Christianity is the middle of the three Abrahamic religions. The same core theme will be repeated in all of them if one looks carefully for the commonality in the respective scriptures. There is a beautiful verse in the Holy Quran (2:256): "There is no compulsion in religion" meaning, do not force anyone to become Muslim, for Islam is plain and clear, and its proofs and evidence are plain and clear (Quran.com). We should embrace this religious tolerance, be proud and confident of our respective faiths, but do not force our views and faith on others.

Everyone thinks that he or she knows better. It is the same reason for writing this book too! It is the author's ego that is writing this book as if to say, 'I know better than others!' It is author's humble request and hope that any of author's personal shortcomings should not tarnish this pristine knowledge. Please read on and try to understand the intricacies of spirituality and try to understand your true nature. Pass on the idea to others if you like, with the caption "I like 'M-Mème'; I suggest you read it too", but do not make this a topic of debate or try to prove it wrong, which can create more friction within you or in the society.

GOD AND RELIGION

Traditionally most of us are led to believe in God and participate in various rituals that form a part of our living. Most of us look up to something beyond the perceived, especially in difficult times. Most of us are brought up with the idea that God is somewhere up there and will punish us if we behave badly. We are also taught that we must pray to God, do good things, etc. Wherever one is born and follows whichever religion, the above is a common sentiment.

God and religion are unnecessarily linked with politics and are resulting in spreading hatred, fear, and causing an enormous amount of damage across the globe, across millennia. In this information age where knowledge is available at the fingertips one should get to the bottom of one's respective religious scriptures and see what the core teachings are. Let us try to look at the oneness in different religions. *Vasudhaika kutumbakam*, meaning all the world is one family, is not just a slogan by a scholar. It is the ultimate Reality.

With so many religions and religious practices around, so many temples, churches, masjids, so many scriptures, so many preachers and *gurus*, telling seemingly different things, it is confusing and misleading. Whatever religion one is born into or following, he/she will passionately believe that his or hers is the only God and all the other religions, and their respective gods are not correct. Anyone who is on the spiritual path must sooner or later realize that God is one, no matter which religion or sect one belongs to.

Let us start with Hindu religion. Bhagavad Gita is one of the most important scriptures for Hindus. It is believed to be narrated by Lord Krishna (God Incarnate) himself. In the Gita, Lord Krishna clearly mentions that he is the father of the universe. When he assumes the "*Vishwaroopa*", Arjuna could see the entire universe in Lord Krishna. When Lord Krishna is the father of the entire universe, people of other religions are also bound to be a part of him, isn't it? Someone born in USA, UK, UAE, Africa, whether they know about Lord Krishna or not, is still part of the same universe that Lord Krishna says he is the father of. Some people may just be oblivious to their parents for a variety of reasons.

According to Christianity, all humanity came from Adam and Eve. If so, people all over the world are the offspring of Adam and Eve, isn't it? Islam says Allah is the creator of the universe. If so, everyone on earth is created by Allah only! Whether someone believes in Allah or not; follows Islam or not, he/she is still created by Allah. Isn't that so? It beggars belief that Gods of different religions are sitting up there, maybe in different corners of the universe, creating people of a particular religion only, putting them on earth, as if there is no other place in the entire universe, and letting them fight with each other to prove their superiority! What if someone changes their religious faith? Do gods have an exchange system? Do you really think your Creator needs your help in upholding his/her name? God does not need your help. God does not have a religion. What is the religion of the Sun, Moon, and Earth? Follow the religion of your choice; do not compare, argue, or impose your views on others. Never try to convert/ change someone's faith. Never be intolerant of other faiths, including the agnostics and atheists.

Whether one understands the above logic or believes in science and anthropology, he/she will come to the same conclusion – God is one. *Advaita* (non-dual) philosophy goes one step further and preaches that the Creator and Creation are one. We will explore this further in a later chapter. People of different faiths may give different names and preach in different ways, but the ultimate Reality is the same. Realized people like Hindu sages, Prophet Moses, Jesus Christ, Prophet Muhammad, Lord Buddha, Nanak Dev gave their accounts based on the time and their geographical location in the language that was prevalent. Part of their teachings is about God and most of it is how to live harmoniously in a society. This again would naturally change according to the time and geographical location of the prophet. Over a period of time, to prove superiority over other regions and religions, the religious houses together with the rulers have come up with various rules and practices of their own. The interpretation of the original teaching has also been changed to suit their propaganda. Fear is the weapon priests and politicians use from time immemorial. The core of all religions depicts God as the most benevolent and pure bliss!

Think of this analogy. Take a city like Delhi. Any traveller who has visited Delhi can write a blog about the city, and how to reach there. The traveller naturally will explain its charm, various places and reasons to visit the place. Obviously, there are a number of means to reach Delhi and each blogger will like a particular way of travel and particular places of interest within Delhi, depending on their own level of understanding, means of travel, their own vocabulary, their ability to express and their target audience. When a city like Delhi or any metropolitan city can have so many ways of expression by so many bloggers, what about the complex topic of God? There are some bloggers who have not visited Delhi but write with the available information on the net about Delhi! Unless you go to Delhi yourself, you will never come to understand what these bloggers are talking about. First thing is to know that such a place exists, then figure out which is the best way for you to reach there and then finally go there. Then you want to write your own blog, adding to the already long list of blogs, which may help some travellers or add to the confusion. Extrapolate this to reaching the entity called God, that cannot be perceived by the senses.

If you trace back the DNA in the maternally inherited mitochondria within our cells, all humans have a theoretical common ancestor. This woman, known as "mitochondrial Eve", lived between 100,000 and 200,000 years ago in southern Africa. If you do not want to agree upon a common religion, at least believe in Anthropology, which states that we all have come from a common ancestor which is proven genetically!

Atheists look to science to prove that there is no God. Some scientists go to enormous lengths to prove that there is no God, as depicted in some religious scriptures, which may not be the correct interpretation to begin with. The scientists unfortunately look at and keep dissecting the observable universe. According to present scientific thought, the observable universe containing billions of galaxies, is only 5% of the total. The remaining 95% is dark matter and energy. There is a lot more than the scientists can dream or think. Ironically, these theoretical scientists are remarkably like the prophets and seers who tried to explain things in nature. Prophets and seers accept the existence of God, whereas the scientists don't. The journey of an ardent scientist-atheist who later turned to spirituality can be found in the book "Believing Is Seeing: A physicist explains how science shattered his atheism and revealed the necessity of faith". The important take-home message in the book is to differentiate between misguided or blind faith and enlightened faith. One must not follow science or religion blindly.

When one reads the books of Sri Stephen Hawking, one of the greatest scientists of our time, one can see a lot of similarities in the way he describes the origin of the universe, multiple histories that a universe can have and the randomness. He goes to extraordinary lengths to explore the universe and prove that there is no God or Creator as depicted in the monotheistic religions. Eastern philosophy has a different view of God, which runs parallel to the observations made by the cosmologists. "The Grand Design", that Sri Hawking mentions as the laws governing the universe, itself is God. Many scientists now agree that the universe as we know and observe, started as the Big Bang, a great explosion of energy. Such an explosion creates a corresponding sound too. Scriptures of *Sanatana Dharma* state that *Adi Shakti* (primordial energy) is the beginning of creation and the universe started from the sound *Om*. The cosmologists' view of the universe being created by a random perturbation (or disturbance) in the quantum vacuum accidentally is in tune with the Vedic view of the origin of creation with a movement in Pure Consciousness depicted as Nirguna Brahman or Shiva or Krishna in unmanifest form. Cosmologists believe that for such an energy to be generated it must be nullified by an equal amount of energy of opposite polarity. These two aspects are depicted as *Shakti* and Shiva or Krishna and *Prakriti* in *Sanatana Dharma*, and Yin and Yang in Chinese philosophy. According to science, there are 7 dimensions curled up in the universe. Multiple histories theory of the universe resonates with what Sri Om Swami says. Is it just coincidence? Or, are different schools of thought describing the same phenomenon? The author is not trying to justify the Eastern philosophy with science. The author is just saying that science is reinventing the wheel and confirming some of the core teachings of Eastern philosophy. Sadly, for various reasons Eastern philosophy has taken a beating and is relegated to the realm of myth and snake charmers. Even many of the preachers and the masses do not know the core of *Sanatana Dharma*. They keep arguing and wondering about *Dvaita* vs. *Advaita*; Vishnu vs. Shiva vs. Shakti, not to mention countless other gods!

In Hinduism almost all things are worshipped, due to the belief (or fact) that "Everything is Divine". Names are given to different energy forms, animals and objects. Over a period of time, the different schools of thought forgot the original scheme and started to figure out who is stronger! The original source of everything manifest is the same – *Adi Shakti*, which is depicted as Supreme Mother. $E = mc^2$. Look at the amount of matter in the manifest cosmos. Add to that the dark matter and energy. Imagine the amount of energy we are talking about. It is that energy worshipped as *Shakti*. Because it is too big a prospect and dangerous to handle it, people have settled on worshipping other energy forms. A good proportion of *Shakti* worshippers also confine the *Adi Shakti* to various embodied forms and names. This is the confusion in Hinduism. One must transcend all the names and forms to realize the Truth.

All the religions come with various stories praising God in different ways. The majority of them are to keep reminding the public about some superior power and to behave well, lest they be punished. They are just to keep up the social order. Some, however, come with a hidden esoteric message which can only be passed on to the disciple by a *Guru*. Most of them are also misinterpreted and misrepresented by people. If you like some story, follow; otherwise, discard. Do not get stuck in a debate whether it is correct or not, with yourself or others.

Corona was a small blip in the grand scheme of things. God does not sit somewhere up there, create Corona and send it to us. Neither does he send the medicine for it. It is all part of nature. How you utilize nature and the time you spend on earth is up to you. Most people have made the concept of God as a thing of convenience. Just visit temple, please God and do whatever nonsense you want to do in the remaining time. It does not work that way.

God is the invisible force permeating the whole universe. God is the energy that drives all of us and everything in the universe. God is a metaphysical phenomenon. God cannot be seen with instruments. You will get a better idea of God if you understand "space". Space is everywhere; starting from the vast outer space to space within us, which is a continuum. The solar system and earth are all suspended in the space only. You may think there is no space within our bodies. Recollect the elementary physics and the structure of the atom. There is a lot of space within each atom. Spirit/Divinity/God is subtler than the space. So don't think you can do things without God knowing. God is a constant companion of everyone, everywhere; simply witnesses what you do.

Action and reaction simply follow the universal laws of *Karma/Dharma*. If you try to understand the grand scheme and try to align with it, your actions will automatically be good and will bring good. Acts done knowingly or unknowingly will bear fruit. It is always better to make a conscious effort.

Author was born into Hindu religion and spent a good amount of childhood in his village temple playing around. Hence most of the thought process is along the lines of *Sanatana Dharma*. The religious festivals that we see today have become a simple show of strength. Devotion has taken a back seat. Whatever devotion that we see is very superficial and short lived. This type of devotion will not take you further in the journey. One needs a deep-rooted devotion and focus. People are happy with the institutions and rituals that are being performed and think that their obligation to God is over. They are too busy in their daily activities that God is a mere convenience or solace.

While we are on the topic of religion, let us look at the definition of religion. It is not just in relation to God. It is a belief or way of living or a school of thought. Some people have made science as their religion. For some travelling, for some gadgets, consumerism! It is not about science or religion or any one subject. It is one's attitude towards it. If you worship and revere science, that becomes your religion. All are important. Everything is important in our life. We should not make any one of them into everything! That is when the problem starts.

For the traditionalists, this may not be palatable. Whether one likes it or not, the Truth does not change. If you continue to be rooted in your traditional beliefs, please continue to do so. Author's purpose is not to argue or prove something, but to make people realize the common thread in our beliefs. In the name of religion and God, people are killing themselves and/or killing others. It is the saddest thing for a human to do. No religion advocates hatred and violence. What the scriptures say about self-defence, people are twisting to use for self-gain, political propaganda and manipulating the gullible into doing heinous things. Some of you may have come to this understanding already. However, it is reiterated as it is one of the first hurdles one must cross in the path of spirituality. If you have an open and receptive mind, it can catch the Truth easily.

RELIGION AND SCIENCE

For generations, science and religion have been at loggerheads. Religion believes in God and science tries to prove that there is no God. It is difficult to understand why some people who don't believe in God are so obsessed with proving there is no God. If scientists want to prove certain misconceptions in the scriptures written thousands of years ago wrong, that is fine. Religion should learn from science and try to accommodate it.

There are some atheists who make science into a religion and are creating gods of their own by adoring the scientists. God is a concept that there is a higher power and is a point of support for many people for a variety of reasons. One should not deprive them of their faith and support system. If you do not believe in God, stay away from such topics. As will be explained later, both believers and non-believers do not know Divinity completely.

Our ancient sages are scientists par excellence. If subsequent generations cannot understand their teachings properly and become misguided, the teachings should not be ridiculed. Modern scientists are seers too. It is just that their tools and focus are different. We owe a lot to both groups. We must try to understand the core of their views and try to make the most of both, rather than arguing and ridiculing each other. Ancient seers are life scientists. They are into physical and metaphysical realms. Modern scientists are focused on the physical realm only.

Prophets, scientists, masters, seers, all are humans only. They will tell what they perceived. Their perception may be flawed in some areas. People want them to know everything and believe blindly what is said. This is the reason for conflict. Take what is said that fits with the observable facts. Decide for yourself which part of the scriptures and to what extent you want to believe. If you blindly follow everything and every misinterpretation, you will end up in conflict and misery. No need to feel bad that your scriptures got a certain aspect wrong. The same applies to scientists. Despite the vast scientific advances, they are still in darkness about the origin of creation and cosmos. Nothing wrong in exploring the universe and evolution. Do not do it to prove that there is no God and to prove the religion wrong. If you do that, you are forming your own religion. Let science be science. Things that cannot be explained for now, leave them; there is no need to prove or disprove God.

Any true scientist is curious and open to suggestions. An astrophysicist will not look at an agricultural scientist doing experiments in a derogatory way and vice versa.

Both have their spheres of interest and expertise. In a similar vein, a true scientist will never be derogatory of metaphysics. They would simply say: It is not my area of interest. Let them do what they are doing. A true scientist or spiritual person is curious, and all efforts are directed towards the betterment of human existence. It is the people who are short-sighted and intolerant of others' point of view that cause the conflict.

Spiritually advanced people may have ignorance in certain areas. They do not want to acknowledge that they are ignorant, as they are supposed to know everything. Whatever path (religion/*Guru*/concept) they followed is a tunnel that gives them tubular vision. They tend to rubbish everything outside their tunnels. The same applies to scientists. Everyone tends to preach their tunnels only. This is the reason for so much confusion and strife. As such, the human mind plays a divisive game and wherever there is conflict, it latches onto it and keeps separating it further. You can see this in the number of divisions present in any religion or scientific thought.

There is no point in science and religion blaming each other. Both are good. Both have limitations. Both have contributed to human well-being and misery. If religions or politicians have started the conflict in the name of God or nation or other causes, science has provided ammunition and technology to annihilate fellow human beings. They should complement each other for the betterment of humankind. Otherwise, (maybe once God's exploration of itself completes), scientists will come up with a G-bomb or nature with some gRNA that will annihilate the world as we know, and the process starts all over again.

Everyone is trying to decipher the universe in their own way. Conclusions of religious seers are based on observing the nature, cosmos, and contemplation. Scientists like Sri Hawking and Sri Dawkins are seers in their own right. They (we) are looking at God in the face but are simply blinded to that fact. They will never be able to realize it unless they calm the incessant activity in their minds - the very thing that took them that far! As long as the mind is oscillating, it won't perceive the Divine. Divine can only be perceived by a 'tranquil mind'.

Science can never answer the question of why a phenomenon happened. It can only answer how. Most of it is by hypothesis, conjecture, and circumstantial evidence. How does it matter to the common person whether primeval soup was there or not? How does it matter whether big bang happened or not? When did it happen? How long the universe is going to last? Can we colonize other galaxies? Leave those things to the scientists. Preachers of religious scriptures and scientists should find a common ground for the betterment of humankind. What matters to us is the present - 'Here and Now'! How can we better our lives?

As already mentioned, the fundamental difference and conflict between religion and science is that religion believes in the existence of a superior power, calls it

God, and gives it various further names. By the way, the word God and various other names are human made. Science does not believe in a superior power but believes that all things are due to natural laws and things have evolved slowly on their own. Both are two sides of the same coin. One cannot see the manifest world with eyes closed. You cannot describe a beautiful sunrise to a blind person. You cannot describe the melody of music to a deaf person. However much you try, they will not be able to appreciate. They must have eyes or ears to appreciate these phenomena. Likewise, one cannot experience the unmanifest with the sense organs. It is a paradox. If you wish to perceive the unmanifest, you must close your eyes, ears, other sense organs, and still the mind. Once you understand the scheme and in the later stages of practice, after having developed enough awareness, closing the eyes and ears is not necessary.

The Unmanifest has no name, no form. It cannot be described. People who have touched that dimension describe it as pure love or bliss. The problem arises when it comes to explaining it to other people. If it is observable by direct observation, it can be described as scientists do. It cannot be described. In trying to explain to other people what they have perceived, the realized person tries in different ways. Other compounding factors are that there are multiple ways to experience the other dimension, and it is not possible to stay in that dimension for long. Most realized people also tend to fall back into the trap of "I" and "mine". This leads to various misinterpretations.

Now that we have scientific facts as well as a compendium of knowledge from various religions, it is high time to amalgamate the ancient wisdom with modern advances. Science alone without spirituality is a disaster. Sticking to religious dogmas and disregarding scientific evidence is also wrong. Enough divisions were created. Enough confusion was generated. Enough fights and wars took place. It is time to reconcile.

Here is a paragraph from the book Selfish Gene: "We have the power to defy the selfish genes of our birth and, if necessary, the selfish Mèmes of our indoctrination. We can even discuss ways of deliberately cultivating and nurturing pure, disinterested altruistic, something that has no place in nature, something that has never existed before in the whole history of the world. We are built as gene machines and cultured as Mème machines, but we have the power to turn against our creators. We, alone on earth, can rebel against the tyranny of the selfish replicators."

As you will see, even the spiritual path is rather selfish to start with. "I" want to be happy, "I" want to realize God, "I" want to be liberated, etc. Our biology is programmed as such in a selfish way. The spiritual path sort of makes one take a U-turn and seek within. As one progresses on the path and loses the conditioning of religion, race, genes, etc., one gets closer to the Divine.

SCIENCE AND SPIRITUALITY

Matter is something we can perceive with our sense organs. It can be demonstrated easily and can be grasped. Spirit is something beyond matter. It cannot be perceived with the sense organs or any of the scientific instruments. Ancient seers have contemplated on this aspect. Their conclusions based on observing nature, cosmos and contemplation are remarkable, to say the least. An average mind and conventional science just look at the material world and try to organize things in the materialistic realm. Spirituality looks at the source of matter and tries to answer the fundamentals of creation, mind and matter together.

Any organism is conditioned with two basic functions: survival and procreation. These two are deep-rooted in any animal, including humans. These manifest as hunger, lust, fear and insecurity, born out of struggle for existence. There are a variety of other negative emotions which again are originally conditioned for survival of the fittest. Over the centuries, these primordial fears and survival instincts have taken a turn for the worse. There is no need for many of these negative emotions as we no longer are the hunter-gatherers and living in jungles. When our understanding of the universe and God was rudimentary, there were a lot of things attributed to God as there was no plausible explanation at that time. Even though we have many advances in science, anthropology, and cosmology, people are still not able to come out of the age-old dogma about God. The religious institutions and politicians wish to continue this dogma and myth out of their own misunderstanding and for their own survival. Remember; your ignorance, fear and greed are the investments of many businesses!

We are drifting further away from nature and the core of our being, which makes us increasingly restless. The restlessness in society is the reason for proliferation of various *yoga* programs and increase in the "religious tourism" these days. This restlessness is also propelling people to cling to various labels, described in a later chapter, as a means of security. Clinging to the labels increases the rift between groups of people having different labels. The labels change but the rift can be seen in almost all walks of life; mine vs not-mine.

A good amount of fear and insecurity in society is unfounded. This is mostly the fear of not being able to acquire or achieve something, or having acquired it, the fear of losing it. With this fear, all the other negative emotions are increasing. Fear is due to a variety of reasons. Not being able to secure a rank in exams, not getting a job that provides enough salary, prospect of falling ill, increasing costs of healthcare, job insecurity, modern lifestyle, and social media buzz with ever-increasing expectations and expenses are some examples.

Apart from the above-mentioned materialistic things, people have become fragile in their sentiments; the smallest of things can upset them and cause mental anguish. It does not take much to hurt the sentiments of someone or some group these days. Many people are psychologically fragile. It manifests in various forms. Because of the fear, people are getting exploited in various ways.

World Health Organization (WHO) defines health as a state of complete physical, mental and social well-being and not merely the absence of disease or infirmity. How many of us fit into this definition these days? Our social media is making us restless, crazy, anxious and fearful most of the time.

If one makes some effort, one can understand that most of one's fears are unfounded. One must make a conscious effort to get over this fear, anxiety and insecurity. If you get rid of the ignorance; fear, anger and other negative emotions fade away. You must be stable, healthy and happy to be able to enjoy life and keep others happy. Slowing down the mad rush that is happening in the mind and society will certainly help. The ultimate possibility of a human being is to understand the working of the mind and sever the shackles of the mind, leading to profound peace and tranquility that is our true nature.

All religions are based on spirituality – metaphysics; study of things beyond the normal sensory perception. It is important to remember that spirituality has no religion. Spiritual path gives you the strength and wisdom to overcome the afflictions of the mind and make yourself a better human being. Spiritual path is the only way out of human misery: individual or collective. One cannot change the entire human race. One can do so for oneself. Do it if you want to. We need people who are fearless, righteous and altruistic in society, especially in the political and bureaucratic spheres. It is difficult to live that way in our society, but it is possible. You may not become a Buddha, but if you make the effort, you will definitely become a better person.

All the religions and spiritual paths lead to one Truth. Despite that, misinterpretations and dogmas are leading to considerable disharmony and suffering in the name of God. All the religions depict God as benevolent and pure bliss. There is no place for suffering in the lap of God. It is our own mind that is separating us from God, creating conflict and misery.

Most of the religious practice these days is out of fear or casual. Religious gatherings are like a show of strength and mass hysteria. People may get some kick out of the events but are not getting the true benefits of spirituality. People are simply getting exploited by the religious industry. True spirituality gives you enormous strength, fearlessness, and profound peace. Get out of frivolous religious madness and follow the core spirituality, whatever may be your religion.

The toolmaker always feels that his/her tool is better and tries to promote it. Some tools may be better than others. But that should not be a reason for us to fight over the tools when all the tools have the same purpose, and the destination is the same. Use tools of any religion to advance your spiritual quest. Any truly God-realized person knows that all is one. If more people understand what Divinity truly is, there will be less mischief that is being done in the name of God.

First step in spirituality is to cultivate inquisitiveness to know more about that metaphysical phenomenon. Second is to acquire knowledge and understand the oneness of creation. Third and final step is to experience and be one with the creation. Very few people reach and remain in the third stage. The majority of religious teachings are for the people at the lower rungs of Maslow's pyramid. Do not get stuck there. Most religions teach how to reach the Ultimate. These are usually given in a cryptic way and need to be pursued specifically.

For people who are on the spiritual path, all this may sound familiar. That is because of two reasons. One is the commonality in all spiritual teachings. Second is a good amount of this knowledge is handed down by various people in different ways. Countless people have been saying the same thing, in different ways.

Following is purely the author's interpretation: Our body is a chemical factory. To sustain life and maintain bodily functions, lot of biochemical processes are involved. The body maintains the equilibrium by various neurohumoral processes and molecules. Some of these molecules are involved in the pain/pleasure perception and our mood/psychology. The capacity to produce all the chemicals is inherent in all of us; unless one has any genetic abnormality. The chemicals produced in the body are based on a complex interplay of what we eat, breathe, think and our genetic predisposition. What we seek and consume in terms of food and other bodily sensations is again dependent on our innate nature, the tendencies. Now that we have the basic knowledge of how the human body and mind works, let us see how that can be translated into our spiritual quest. All of us have the chemical factory that is required to give happiness. As the scenes unfold in our life, the mind keeps analysing and reacting based on its preconceived notions. These reactions; mental or physical, pave way for further scenes in our life. The mind always seeks pleasure and or security. All the analysis and reaction by the mind is centred around pleasing oneself or being safe. All the while the chemical factory in the body is either the cause or effect of our actions and emotions. Mind wants some accomplishment and a sense of achievement. It is seeking to produce the "feel-good" chemicals. Some of these feel-good chemicals like psychedelics are available in nature or can be manufactured in the lab and can give the same effect. However, the natural design of the body is such that whatever accomplishment and the effect of the feel-good chemicals (innate or as psychedelics), is short lived. The psychedelics simply take one to the state of mindlessness which is very similar to transcending the mind by proper spiritual practice. Everyone knows that the externally administered feel-good chemicals are habit forming, counterproductive and dangerous. When the mind is bored by a particular accomplishment, it seeks another thing. It wants more and more chemicals. Several philosophers have looked into this phenomenon and figured out ways of achieving lasting feel-good chemicals. There are many ways of doing it. As part of the spiritual practice, our job is to conduct our life in such a way that we channel our energies and efforts to produce more of the desired chemicals. In this process, we take the help of an external agency in the form of *Guru* or God. However, mind prefers short-cuts and quick gratification by sensual pleasures than the hard way of spiritual practice and keeps us distracting towards various material things.The state of lasting bliss may be achieved at some point by a shift in the perception of the mind and the subsequent alteration in the chemicals produced.

TEMPLES AND ASTROLOGY

Lot of emphasis is given to places of worship in religions. When it is said that God is everywhere, what is the need of places of worship? You need a place for focusing and contemplation. Hence the place of worship. Use them to the extent necessary. Preserve them, but do not go overboard to prove that your particular place of worship is better than others. People must realise that God does not stay in the places of worship only or in any particular place. It is good to visit places of worship to remind us about God and to give some tranquillity. Many places are anything but tranquillity these days. Do not make places of worship noisy. If going to a place of worship gives you calmness of mind, please do go. There is some energy in these places of worship – either geographical or the way they are constructed or the collective energy of the disciples. Either way they are good, provided going there and spending time there is done with reverence and contemplation rather than just a chore. If you cannot visit a place of worship for whatever reason, do not allow it to create negative thoughts in you.

Hindu temples are built as per *Agama Shastra* and *Vaastu Shastra*. All the major temples are built at a specific place for a specific purpose. They are consecrated as per the rituals. Places of worship belonging to other religions also have rituals and processes of building the place. Try to know the purpose of that particular place and its history while visiting. Follow the rules set out by those who established that place. Do not use your rationalism and try to disobey the rules. Do not desecrate any place of worship. Remember, all the places of worship, irrespective of religion are to be revered in the same way. Never think that God is in this place only. Think God is in this place also. God is omniscient, not confined to a particular place of worship.

People have gotten into the mindset that if they give gifts to God, they will receive gifts in return. In their own greed, show of wealth and self-glorification, people are spending a lot of money on religious events and on places of worship. We must support the places of worship. But do not go overboard and make it an obscene display. Know that helping a downtrodden person, feeding a hungry person or educating a poor child is equally good, if not better.

Astrology is an important aspect of Hindu religion. Future predictions are a part of all cultures. Humans are always curious to know what the future holds. Predictions of some like Sri Veera Brahmam, Sri Nostradamus or Baba Vanga are accurate to some extent. It is always intriguing how a person can tell someone's life events by looking at the birth chart or humanity in general with relative accuracy. We all know that our lives along with the rest of nature are intricately linked to the movement of Earth, Sun and Moon. The key is perhaps in Quantum Gravity and Quantum Biology; they may be able to explain the effects of planetary movements on individuals. As discussed in the chapter on *Karma*, if we come with our source code, may be they have the know-how to decipher that source code. In the hands of people with correct knowledge and intuition, Astrology maybe considered as a science. But be aware that the predictions are not accurate, for various reasons. Or perhaps more importantly, we can change the future! If our life is predetermined, what is the point of going through all the effort? We must not resign ourselves based on Astrology or *Karma* or any other predictions. We should not allow them to weaken our mind.

Whatever your beliefs may be, if you wish to follow them, please do. Two things need to be emphasized. Do not argue with people about the greatness of your beliefs or prove that your beliefs are correct. Do not let your beliefs (or people based on your beliefs) blackmail you and lead to negativity. We can change our fate or destiny by making proper effort. That effort and the ability to change our future are available only in the present moment or day. Do not ruminate over the past, procrastinate or worry over the future. Develop awareness and try to do proper activities to take life in the direction that you want. Your focus should be on improving yourself today. Do mindful activities within the moral and ethical limits of the society you live in and try to make way for a better future for yourself and for the society in general.

DIVISION AND UNION

We all want everlasting happiness in life. However, it seems to elude most people, including the rich and famous. The human mind is divisive. It always tries to separate things and tries to do better, improvise and innovate. That in itself is not a bad thing. Without which we would not have all the development in various fields. The problem comes when the human mind and body drift too far away from the source of its existence and nature. The more it tries to overcome the natural phenomena and to please itself with material comforts in the pursuit of happiness, the more unhappy it becomes.

The word *Yoga* means union. There are a variety of methods or paths to remove the divisiveness of the mind and unite the individual consciousness with that of the universal. Of the various paths in *yoga* – *Bhakti*, *Karma*, *Kriya* and *Jnana* are the main ones. The different types of *yoga* are not exclusive; these can be and are better used in combination. On close scrutiny one will find *Bhakti* and *Kriya* also to be part of *Karma* only. The popular *yoga* programs and what is preached in the present-day spirituality groups are only a small portion of the entire gamut of *yoga*. Amrita Gita of Swami Sivananda is a small book that explains all the different types of *yoga*.

Bhakti yoga is the path of devotion, which forms the basis of all religions. Devotion means extreme and utter devotion, as shown by Meera Bai or Kannappa. One who follows this path should accept everything as the doing of God. These days God is more of a convenience for quick solace in times of difficulty and can be pleased by offering some prayers or money or material offerings at the place of worship. That is a lower level of *bhakti*, not *Bhakti yoga*, which is utter devotion, accepting everything as godly and offering everything to God, no room for 'I' or the ego, I-ness. There are various types of *Bhakti*, elucidated well in treatises called Narada Bhakti Sutras and Shandilya Bhakti Sutras.

Some of you may be familiar with *Sri Krishna Tulabharam*, a story in Srimadbhagavatam. Satyabhama, one of Krishna's wives gives him away to Narada as part of a ritual, with the proviso that she can get Krishna back by giving Narada an equivalent weight of goods. When the time comes to weigh Krishna, all the material wealth that Satyabhama possessed does not match the weight of Krishna. In desperation she runs to Rukmini, another wife of Krishna. Rukmini prays to Krishna and places a twig of a sacred plant on the scales that weighs more than Krishna. Narada takes the twig and gives Krishna back to Rukmini. This story illustrates the importance of devotion. People try to offer God many material things to show off their devotion. Whose material is it to begin with that you are offering? It is not the material that is important. It is the amount of devotion that matters as the above story illustrates. Also, there is an allusion to mind and matter in this story. Think about it.

Whether it is good or bad or ugly, happening to oneself or others, it should be seen as the handiwork of God. You may be familiar with the phrases: *Ishwarechha* and *Inshallah*; both connote the same meaning. As mentioned in the earlier section, one should believe, accept and embrace all the religions; everything emanated from the same God, whatever religion one may choose to follow, whatever name one may want to pray to. One should perform their duties to the best of their abilities in utter humility and as an offering to their chosen God. This level of devotion is not possible to many people, especially this day and age when our egos are so inflated and busy with material things. The mind keeps coming in the way constantly with its preconceived notions, prejudices and judgments.

Karma yoga is the path of doing. This is more suitable to the present day. The principle behind this is that every action (*Karma*), mental or physical, one performs comes back and one must enjoy or suffer the results and repercussions of one's actions some time in the future, which is as simple as Newton's third law. One should perform the actions according to his/her role in the society – as a child, as a householder, as a professional. There will be some conflict of interest at times, but one should choose the righteous action. The catch in this path is that one should perform the actions as required, without getting attached to the results of the actions. It is not so easy to achieve. After all, we do things for either personal gain, satisfaction or recognition. *Karma* is the crux of the workings of the cosmos. We will look at it in some detail in the next chapter.

Kriya yoga is to channel the life energies in the body by keeping the body in certain postures (*Hatha yoga*) and practicing breathing (*Pranayama*). This is easy to follow in the beginning as all one needs to do is simply follow the set of steps (*Kriya*) as taught. One will notice a great deal of benefit initially, as can be seen by the popularity of the many *Kriya* techniques available. *Tantra yoga* practices activate the *Kundalini*, the dormant energy in everyone, and help one achieve the highest level of transcendence. However, if one wants to go all the way using *Kriya* or *Tantra*, guidance by a proper *Guru* is necessary.

Mantra yoga is done by chanting a particular *Mantra* and the prescribed rituals. *Japa yoga* is repeating any God's name or *Mantra*. Each *Mantra* has a specific purpose. The science behind them is that the sound while chanting them with correct intonation generates vibrations, which helps in achieving the purpose. Remember, the creation started with sound. One should be initiated by a *Guru* for proper use of them. There are some simple mantras in common usage. One of them is "*Om Namah Shivaya*", regular internal chanting of which can help.

Neuroscientists have come up with the idea of "Default mode neural network" for certain disorders of the brain. This actually is true for all our brains; disease or no disease. The mind tends to slip back into the same patterns despite attempts to change it. Spiritual practices, especially *Mantra yoga* and meditation aim to change those default networks and tendencies of the brain. However, you must be careful about what you want out of it and guided properly. Otherwise, you may go off course in the spiritual maze and end up in blind alleys. More information can be found in books by Sri Om Swami (Black Lotus) on the topic.

Jnana yoga is developing the awareness and discrimination. This is purely a mental exercise. One must constantly be on the watch, observe and analyze. Not just what is happening all around, but 'within' is more important. Observing oneself, mainly the thoughts arising and keeping constant "awareness" is the key. We will explore more on this in the next chapters.

As mentioned earlier, these are not exclusive of one another. For example, what Lord Buddha taught is a combination of *Karma* (*Dharma*) and *Jnana* (Awareness). The main problem in the past and continuing in the present is people trying to decide which path is better and bickering with each other that their path is better. If one gets into this debate either with oneself or with others, the spiritual journey will not progress. One simple example is: chanting of "*Om*". If you ask for the reason to chant it, you are given a variety of reasons.

You either believe any one of them and get on with the chanting, or keep dissecting the reasons and try to figure out which is the correct reason and get lost in the maze!

Spiritual path is not "inaction" or escapism. Work should not affect spiritual practice. Spiritual practice should not affect work. One must balance among various things: material vs spiritual, family/friends vs connecting with self, progress vs containment, religion vs science, acquiring vs renunciation, doing vs non-doing. One must choose the path of action and mental renunciation.

There are many things that are still out of common comprehension. Such as previous births, rebirth, life after death, twin flames, past life regressions, why some people do not get punished despite a lot of wrongdoing, why innocent people like children suffer, social justice, etc. What is the purpose of the creation itself? People have come up with different ideas. If you like those, believe them. If you do not like those ideas or concepts, do not believe. Do not let your beliefs or disbeliefs get into conflict with yourself or others. The whole idea is to better ourselves and those around us in this very life. What we do know is that it is possible by correct spiritual practice.

The core of spiritual journey is oneness and the removal of the divisive game of the mind. One must understand that everything emanates from the same Source and spiritual journey is the process of uniting the individual consciousness with the universal consciousness. It is not an easy task. It is a very arduous path, especially if one has to perform the regular householder duties. One must keep track of the progress and not get entangled in the various paths and teachings.

Do not worry too much about past or future lives, or hypothetical heaven or hell after death. Why are you bothered about life after death? That you will never know! Your physical body is not going anywhere after death. You will not be here to tell the experiences of heaven or hell. Look around. They are here: around us and in your own mind. If you accept, understand and rise above your petty mind, heaven is only here. You can enjoy the supreme bliss, which is unique and second to none! You may consider all this as a process of self-hypnosis or psychotherapy; it is not. Even so, is it not better to do this way than going through the roller coaster of emotions or ending up taking medicines for uncontrolled emotions?

For some people, living itself is a struggle. We cannot teach them formal spirituality. They also can turn to some higher power (God) for guidance or strength. Many people are walking the path without knowing. Some of them do it better than the *gurus*. Who taught Kannappa spirituality? People who are simple, obey nature, live in harmony with nature, take things as they come and are happy as they are, do not need formal education in spirituality; they are spiritual as they are. Spiritual path is for people who want more! It is also for people who want to overcome the negative emotions in life.

People are trying to exploit nature and other people's weaknesses and are in turn getting exploited by others. The author strongly urges people who are educated, have "achieved" something in life to write a bucket list of things to do at some point in life while they still have the energy and complete the bucket list. As you will see for yourself, the desires keep coming, bucket list after bucket list. At some point, you must curtail your desires and turn to serious spiritual seeking. There are countless people who are bored, directionless and fearful in their advanced age.

We have the capacity to unravel the mysteries of the universe and creation. In doing so, if we can get to the bottom of things, we can touch a totally different dimension. Our seers have done it and shown the path. It is up to us whether to travel the path and know for ourselves. Our senses and science stop at the physical (material) level of the manifest universe. You need metaphysics (spirituality) to go beyond.

Once you are on the path, you must prove to yourself and to others that you are "above" the ordinary crowd. Otherwise, it is just armchair spirituality and even escapism! It puts additional strain on the resources (energy body) that we have. With constant practice, this can be overcome; one feels more energetic and freer with passing of time.

Reconcile the differences - religious, nationalist, sects, etc. Enormous damage is being done to humanity and the planet as a whole - animate and inanimate. Spare a thought for the food, goods, and everything you are using. Try to live as harmoniously as possible with nature. This cannot be done at once by everyone. Start individually and, hopefully, one day the community will change.

One can judge one's progress. This is most important. Do not get stuck in the rut of faith or spirituality without progressing! Over a period of time there will be a lessening of the negative emotions - fear, anger, jealousy, resentment, greed and lust. The positive emotions will rise - happiness, contentment and joy which hopefully one day culminate in the Bliss Absolute.

KARMA – DHARMA

It is the idea that our life depends on our deeds, past and present. Both Hindu religion and Buddhism highlight this aspect. The deeds are all the activities done knowingly or unknowingly and include thoughts as well. It is a no-brainer that you will get results for your labour. There is mention of it in the Bible too: "You reap what you sow" (Galatians 6:7–9). The entire universe runs on the law of causality. The present depends on the past activity and the future depends on the cumulative activity of past and present. Sometimes this simple law of cause and effect doesn't seem to be working properly, as some of the happenings in one's life cannot be explained in one's lifetime; hence the concept of past lives and future lives is considered. For example, a seemingly pious person running into problems and vice versa. Whether you believe in past and future lives, you can certainly believe in the concept of your future being the result of your own actions rather than some form of determinism. Do not be entangled in the concepts of afterlife, heaven, hell and next life. We will never know about any of those with our present body or mind. Be focussed on the present life – here and now! Make this life better in all possible ways. See the results in this very life!

In a nutshell, you create your own source code or script for your life. Everyone of us has a store of code called the "*Sanchita karma*". We take a part of it (*Prarabdha karma*) as a script for this birth, which decides our parentage, personal attributes, other relationships and the society we are born into. This perhaps forms the basis of predictions by astrologers based on location and time of birth. This is mentioned in another chapter. As we spend life we enjoy or suffer according to the fructification of the past *karma*. What we do in the present life (moment) is the *Agami karma*. Some of the *Agami karma* fructifies in this life itself, which can be seen as success or failure of what and how you do things. Some of the *Agami karma* that is not fructified in this life is added to the *Sanchita karma*. All this information (our actions, emotions, memories and tendencies) is stored in our subtle body which transmigrates, and the cycle goes on. The memory of identity is wiped off at the time of rebirth. There is no one keeping tabs on us and directing us to hell or heaven in afterlife. Your subtle body may spend some time in the astral world, which cannot be seen, and comes back with another birth. As you can see, we have control over the *Agami karma* only; and as you will see in the next chapter, the window is very narrow.

All your present situations are based on your past activities. Think of it this way: your relationships are dependent on your past *karma*, either this life or a previous life! The set of parents and the social circumstances are based on your past *karma*. Your biggest past *karma* perhaps comes in the form of your spouse! That is probably the reason for the saying "Marriages are made in Heaven". You cannot really go back in a time machine and change your past. So, accept them as they are. Accept everything, without anger or resentment. No point ruminating over the past. Forgive yourself and forgive others. This does not mean you should forget your past. You must use the past only to make better decisions in the present. As you will see in the "Present moment" chapter, there is a very narrow window between past and future. Your past tendencies and impressions will drive you towards the set pattern. It is up to you to understand the system, overcome the tendencies and try to change the course of your life. You must be very attentive and act in the present, otherwise life follows determinism or fate. If your actions are in line with your fate, it goes on autopilot. If you want to change things and steer your life in a different way, you must make the effort in the present.

Karma, the kind of action one does, is classified as *satkarma* (good deeds), *dushkarma* (bad deeds) and *nishiddha karma* (prohibited deeds). If you do good deeds, you get back good results and vice versa. It is the motive behind the action that counts rather than the action itself. It is bad *karma* to kill someone. However, a soldier killing in battle as duty without harboring personal ill will towards the enemy, will not incur bad *karma*. That belongs to the generals or politicians making the decision to go to war and the collective *karma* of the country that goes to war. If your actions are proper and done with good intentions at heart, they will bear good fruits. Even the good *karma* leads to bondage. If you perform the actions just for the sake of action as a responsibility, without any expectations of the result and attaching yourself to the results, it makes way for liberation! This is the *Karma yoga*.

The *Karma* concept essentially puts you on center stage. You are responsible for everything happening in your life. Whatever you are cognizing as an individual or society, the script was written by yourself or yourselves in the past; perhaps a few lifetimes back or just a moment ago. The script is just being played out. The results may be seen moments later or lifetimes later. As mentioned above, the script is re-written on the go depending on the actions of the individual; both physical and mental. This script goes on as a hyperloop with birth and death as intermediary stations. Maybe with an interlude in heaven or hell based on your belief. For one to get off the hyperloop, one needs to make effort in the present life. All the code (*Karma*), except *Prarabdha*, is wiped off if you get the correct knowledge and then the cycle ends. This is what is called liberation or *moksha*. This is what almost all the Eastern seers talk about. The person who has the correct knowledge (*Jnani*) will continue to live life according to *Prarabdha* until the body perishes. You can search the web or read the books on the topic by Swami Tatvavidananda Saraswati and Sri Vee Jay Attri.

PRESENT MOMENT

The author has practiced all the types of *yoga* mentioned in the previous chapters and found all of them to be helpful to some extent. Close scrutiny will reveal that all the techniques eventually aim to calm the restless mind and reach a state of "tranquil mind". However, what helped the author most was the concept of "observing the observer", being in the present moment and developing "Awareness". It will be expanded further here. If you wish to read the original detailed text, please read "Power of Now" by Sri Eckhart Tolle and the books of Sri Jiddu Krishnamurti.

The concept (a fact really) is that our mind is never in the present moment. It keeps oscillating between past and future. Here you must understand the very narrow window between past and future. Just as an illustration, consider the following:

Read the following sentences one after the other slowly.

This is your present moment. Line one is in the past. Line 3 is in the future.

This is now the present. Line 2 is in the past. Line 4 is in the future.

This is now the present. What was the future a moment ago is now the present. The next moment is the future.

As you can see, we do not stay in the present for long. Chronologically, it is a split second. Past and future are simply projections of the mind. They are not real. Only the present moment is real. The mind keeps oscillating between the past and the future. Even as you are reading this, your mind will have some background noise of the past or the future. The idea of staying in the "Now" is to still the mind and increase our awareness of the present moment.

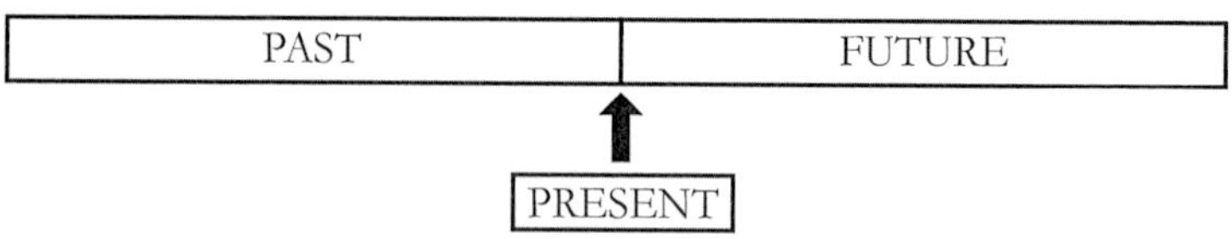

What is normally a split second can be extended. If we extend our present moment, it reduces the mind's projections of past and future.

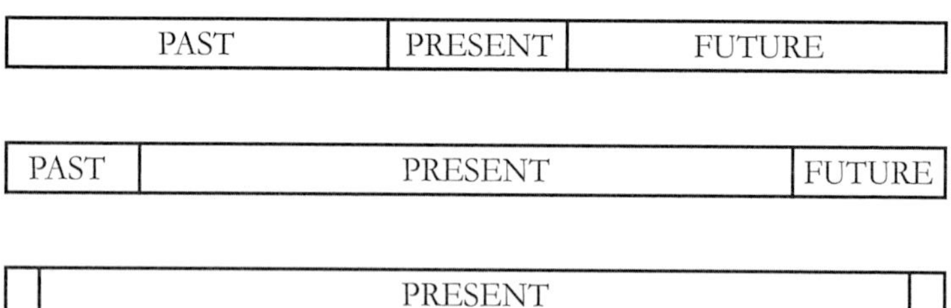

If you are in the present completely, you have attained the liberated state of Timelessness...

To overcome the division in your mind, create another partition and allocate a part of your mind just to observe. Just experiment with this idea. Develop a split mind. Core or inner mind should be the observer, judge, and director of your outer mind, which does the interaction with the outer world. The core should be devoid of any prejudices or identifications. It should be an impartial observer of the situation and direct the outer mind.

It is not so easy. Develop a "me" time. In that time, contemplate whether your outer mind and body are working properly, your life is going in the correct direction and what corrections need to be made. Never take snap decisions. Simply contemplate, analyze and take course correction measures. Whether it is your job, relationships, or spiritual practices, keep observing and analyzing yourself. The core mind should not get perturbed by anything. It is just an impartial observer and a guide to the outer mind. The inner mind should direct the outer mind regarding the discipline of the body, eating, job performance, etc. Unless the body is relatively comfortable and the outer mind is satiated, they will not listen to the inner mind. The inner mind should try to have more time to contemplate. Slowly you will see the change for yourself. The inner mind should try to connect with your (our) source, universal consciousness, which is the actual witness of everything that is happening in the universe.

Keep observing what is happening to your body, outer mind and your life in general by following a path. The way to do it is to observe your every activity and thought arising – being the observer. This should be started initially while sitting in silence and contemplation. Simply observing the thoughts arising. Just observing them without giving any importance, being judgmental or getting entangled in them.

Keep observing your thoughts about everything happening around. Most of the information we receive is absolutely useless for us. But the mind keeps forming judgments and making stories around the external events. Remind yourself what is not necessary for you and stop your mind from wandering. Your mind may wander due to events in the memory also. Either way, you need to constantly keep reminding yourself and rid yourself of the unnecessary thoughts. Do not get frustrated if your mind keeps wandering despite your efforts. It is the nature of the mind to keep wandering. Do not get upset and let the mind create new stories. Simply observe and keep reminding yourself that the stories are not necessary.

More than 95% of the time one sits in meditation, especially in the early stages, the mind goes hither and thither. The design of the mind is like that - a monkey; maybe monkeys are more stable! For brief periods, it calms down. Very occasionally one may get a flash of an out-of-the-world (out of the mind) experience. Don't get frustrated by the unruly monkey mind or get elated by out-of-the-world experiences. Your experience may be different from others'. Don't compare. Just observe.

Slowly, you will notice that you have better control over your mind and its ways of working. Concentrate on important things in your life. As the inner transformation happens, you will notice that your response to external situations is slowly changing. People around you may also notice the change in you. It is a slow process. Do not be in a hurry. Keep doing your spiritual practices. Keep reading and listening to scriptures. Do not get fooled by the inadequacies in the explanation of the scriptures by the scholars or your inability to understand the scriptures fully. Keep observing your thoughts and workings of your mind. Keep reminding yourself that you are not simply the material body or the mind you perceive. You are the ever-present witness. As you progress, you will notice a certain inner calmness. Keep going.

Sri Jiddu Krishnamurti calls it choiceless awareness. Slowly, this can be extended to the daily activities and to the happenings in our life, to look at them as specific patterns and try to break them. Try to abide in the gap between thoughts.

When your mind fully settles into a thoughtless state, you will come to know what this is all about. In that silence, you may find some answers. In the "Subject-Object" (Seer-Seen) relationship, subjective cognition is necessary for the object to exist. Our psyche runs after the object and tries to explore it and have some interaction with it. One must understand that the cognizing principle (Subject) gives existence to all the objects, which is the manifest world in all its glory and all the interactions one has. When this is recognized, all the objects, including one's body and mind, merge into the subject, which is the ever-witnessing consciousness. It is complete transcendence of duality and losing the "I-ness" completely. Possible only for a few out of millions of seekers. This is explained in great detail by Sri Sankara in "Drik-Drisya Vivekam". Sri Jiddu's discussion is also on similar lines. One can see the close parallels in quantum physics; Young's double-slit experiment provides profound insight into the wave-particle duality and how it is affected by the observer.

NON-DUALITY (*ADVAITA*)

Until now we looked at various concepts to channel the energy in the body by doing some form of work (*Bhakti*, rituals, *kriyas*, regular work), how to be aware of our thoughts, modulate our mind and thereby calm the mind. There are further concepts that are not dealt with in this book. All of these concepts are based on Duality, meaning a person (you, author, anyone) is a separate entity and that he or she should do something to better life in the material world or on the spiritual path. This is what everyone perceives - I am an individual. I want a better life, I want more money, I want power, I want fame, I want to learn more, I want to do good, I want liberation etc. The division in the mind mentioned in earlier chapters results in the duality.

Welcome to the concept of "*Advaita*" – non-duality. It is the essence of Vedanta: the Upanishads. This concept states that you are not a separate entity, you (and everyone else) are a part of the Whole. You just perceive yourself as a separate entity due to the veil of ignorance in your mind. If you remove that veil of ignorance, you will be one with the Whole. The major difference in *Advaita* compared to other schools of thought and even common perception is that, according to *Advaita* the separation is not real; it is just perceived. Common perception and all other schools of thought are that you are separate from the Source, and you must do something to unite with the Source. *Advaita* says there is only one Being. All manifestation happens only in that Being. It is one's own ignorance that makes one feel separate – the separation is apparent, not real.

There are various analogies to prove the point and how to overcome the veil of ignorance. One of the analogies is the ocean and the waves. We all are different waves in the same ocean. *Advaita* advocates not identifying with the wave but with the ocean itself. By expanding the consciousness beyond the wave, one becomes the all-encompassing ocean.

The core teaching of *Advaita* revolves around the fact that every one of us knows that we exist. We do not need any proof that we exist. We all say all the time "I am". *Advaita* seizes that point and asks one to hold on to that single thought – "I am". It is the proof of your own existence and that of God, resonating with Exodus 3:14, "I am that I am".

However, this base thought gets corrupted by the veil of ignorance, which is one's own "ego", and confines itself to the body/mind complex, thereby creating the subsequent thoughts of I and mine. Don't get confused with the word "ego", which is used in an "egoistic" sense. In spiritual parlance, it is the feeling of I-ness with which you identify yourself. The "I am" doesn't stop there. It continues as "I am, so and so." It is always attached to a label like: I am a father, a mother, an Indian, a Hindu, a doctor, etc.

Ego or I-ness is your subtle body that carries all the past impressions and tendencies we discussed in the *Karma* chapter. It acts as a prism and skews the perception of the person. One simple example is: imagine going to a shop (or any other place) with a couple of your friends. By seeing some object or a scene, each one of you will react differently. It is the impressions on your mind that condition your response to any given situation. This is too simple an example. Volumes have been written about the workings of the mind and ego as this forms the crux of the spiritual journey.

What you, the author, and everyone think as "I" and the consequent "Mine", is considered in the Vedantic terms as the "false I". The author calls it the "Baby I". False I or the baby I indeed is the ego, or the veil of ignorance that gives the feeling that one is separated from the Whole. The baby I confines itself to the body and a few things that it considers "Mine". The baby I adds various labels to it as part of its existence. First label is "I am so and so (name)". Next are the relations and others. Some are natural and some are acquired. The labels are the various hats/masks we apply to ourselves by means of relationships (father/mother, brother/sister, son/daughter, friends etc), or job-related (I am a doctor/I am a surgeon or I work for a certain hospital or company), belonging to a particular community, state, country, or social clubs, etc. These labels are further augmented by our parenting, education, and our own experiences.

The ego (baby I) feels restless due to the real or apparent separation from its Source. As mentioned in the previous chapters, it tries to overcome that restlessness by various material things. It finds a sense of security in clinging to various labels described above, to different relationships, acquiring wealth, power, knowledge, and various other means. Anything that is outside the confines of the baby I and its 'Mine' is considered as alien, causing polarization and friction. This is the basis of conflict. This conflict at societal level is augmented by religion, politics, and nationality. Some of these labels are necessary for our survival and community living. But one must understand that it is the polarization based on different labels that is the root cause of conflict at individual, societal, and national level.

One must transcend all these labels in spirituality, including the spiritual labels. In theory, it may sound simple, or even absurd to the uninitiated. In practice, it is very difficult to get rid of the ego, the I-ness, false I, or the baby I. It clings dearly to various things as it fears annihilation. Directly or indirectly, all the spiritual practices, especially the meditations are aimed at reducing the ego only. Sri Jiddu Krishnamurti rubbishes all these practices and proposes: "Can you not analyze your thoughts, go to the root of the thought process and drop your ego?" What he proposes is the ultimate *Jnana* path. Not everyone has the incisive mind and discriminatory power of Sri Jiddu. Many people think that Sri Jiddu doesn't believe in God. It is not true. Analyze his words carefully. He points to that one Divinity only. His book "You are the world" resonates with the *Advaita* Vedanta's "You are That"! Look for the commonality; it takes you to the Truth. When ego or the baby I is transcended or annihilated, what remains is the real I in the "I am". It is the Whole, it is Existence, which is our true nature, the "Absolute Being".

The journey starts in duality; one must read the scriptures, try to purify the body and mind as prescribed to receive the final teaching from an enlightened *Guru*. These days it is very difficult to find a genuine *Guru*. However, if your *Sadhana* is sincere and your seeking is ardent, the *Guru* will manifest in your life. As Swami Sivananda pointed out, "the best *Guru* is within oneself"; the pristine "I am". You must follow the practice, the most important aspect is "self-restraint". There is nothing outside. You just need to overcome your own ignorance and your own ego.

Ego is such a cunning thing that it doesn't want to go away. It comes with various disguises. On the spiritual path, it poses as "I am pious", "I have built temples", "I have performed *Yagas*", "I have donated to charity", "I have read all the scriptures", "I want to read more scriptures", "I have helped people on spiritual journey by teaching or writing books", etc. You must be very observant and watch the tendencies of your mind. Otherwise, it lulls you into falsehoods. The mother of all is "I am enlightened"!!! In non-duality, "I am enlightened" is an oxymoron. As long as I-ness exists, you have not transcended the duality. Once you are in non-dual realm, there is no one else you can communicate with!

As the thought arises and is verbalized, it is no longer non-dual. All the scriptures, teachings and concepts, including *Advaita*, happen in duality only. Non-duality can only be experienced. Once it is experienced, the person ceases to exist psychologically and usually becomes silent. His/her body will continue to function as per requirement with no psychological attachment. Some masters may speak for the benefit of humanity. The best such examples in living memory are Sri Ramana and Sri Nisargadatta.

Next comes the final twist in "Pure *Advaita*". When all that exists is only the "Being" and you are not a separate entity to begin with, how can you do anything, including the spiritual practices to better yourself? This is the line of thought expressed by Sri Ramana, Sri Nisargadatta, Sri Ramesh Balsekar, Sri Teja Anand, and many modern seers in non-duality spaces on Quora and the web. Without proper understanding, this line of thought is dangerous and makes all the scriptures, spiritual practices, and the lineage of *Gurus*, and even general education redundant.

Let us look at the two schools of thought. The first one is the traditional wisdom and teachings from various ancient Indian seers, Bhagavad Gita, Bible, Quran and all the other scriptures and interpretations by various saints as to how to better oneself in material life and how to attain God. The second school of thought is that you have no control over your life; everything is preordained; meaning destiny or fate. This brings us to the debate of free will vs destiny.

If the second school of thought is correct, why would so many seers from the past go through the trouble of writing the scriptures and passing the knowledge down the generations? The ancient Indian seers have systematized this knowledge and the step-by-step process in an extensive way. The Bhagavad Gita is a good example of this. There is free will as long as the 'baby I' exists, which one can and must exercise.

The second line of thought that all that there is, is "Being" or "Consciousness" and it is playing its dream, is perfectly in sync with the first stanza of Isavasya Upanishad – "*Isavasyamidagam Sarvam*". It is indeed common in all non-duality statements, including that of Sri Sankara in that "There is only Being; no becoming." Meaning: you just got your identification wrong. All that you need to do is remove the false identification. You are already That.

However, the Upanishad *Rishis*, Lord Krishna, Sri Sankara and other seers go on to mention the practice to reach that conclusion and vision. The modern seers are speaking purely from the "other side"; they probably feel that the modern mind is getting lost in the maze of spiritual teachings and practices, and is doing more harm than good. Perhaps that is the reason to take that line of thought. Author's view is that it should be advocated only to people who have purified their bodies and minds by some spiritual practice and austerities towards "Becoming" (getting liberated) before experiencing the "Being". The big advantage of the second school of thought however, is that it removes the ego and free will out of the equation and is a final assault on the ego to make it redundant. It is the "Surrender" that we so often hear in spirituality. In the final stage one should lose the "I want liberation" thought as well. The seeker must no longer be there.

If you can get a good interpretation of Sri Sankara, who is the proponent of *Advaita*, it is of high value. Sri Sankara's teachings are based on his own experience and the Upanishads, which are the final teachings of the Vedas. All are about the Oneness only.

If we think about the origin of creation: it all came from a void. It is not truly a void but unmanifest consciousness. From that came a thought (mind) and thereafter the matter. Mind and matter are also interpreted as word and its meaning; remember Raghuvamsa 1:1 and John 1:1. Together these form the trinity. These are experienced and explained by different seers and scriptures in different ways. Shiva-Shakti-Manifestation, Krishna-Maya-Prakriti, Father-Spirit-Son, and Seer-Seeing-Seen. The Author's interpretation of it is "The dance of I and i (real I and baby I)". Try to understand this equation: I-i - iIi - i-I. In this equation, the first set of I-i is the individual. The last set is whatever the individual is coming in contact with. The middle set is the medium through which the individual is interacting with the perceived other: an individual or the world. If you understand well, it is the real I that is manifesting and interacting through or as the various "baby Is" and the material world.

All the interactions happen at the level of baby I only. Even the realized person has to interact with the world through the baby I. Some just stay silent. Some say we are all the same when the baby I is removed; so, figure it out for yourself. Some prophets and seers are humble and say that "I am the messenger of the real I" and give means and ways to go about it, depending on the scaffold that helped them reach the summit in the form of idols and their *Gurus*, which form the major chunk of scriptures. Some say "I am the real I"and people also treat them like that. The actual work is to be done between your own baby I and the real I. As it is not easy to tell all the "baby Is" in a direct way, so many indirect ways of taming the baby I and the mind have come up. When the duality created by the mind is removed, the matter merges into the spirit. From the purely non-dual perspective, the manifest world is a Dream, *Abhasa*, Illusion, or *Leela* as described by different schools of philosophy.

Oneness is the culmination of one's spiritual journey. It is not easy to achieve, but one can certainly understand the principle and try to evolve as much as one can. A simple and easy-to-grasp non-dual analogy is to consider this materialistic life as a dream. In the dream, you try to do whatever you feel best in your circumstances. When you are in the dream (under the veil of ignorance) you cannot perceive the Reality, even though it is always with you and is your true nature. When you wake up, what you consider real now, becomes the dream. When you are in deep slumber and in your dream world, can anyone wake you up? As it happens, the author writing this book and you reading it are also happening in the dream world.

Try to take the cues, practice, and hope to wake up from the dream one day! All that you can do is, try to understand the concept and work accordingly. In the "Delhi analogy", you are already in Delhi; you just don't know it! That is the view taken by Sri Ramana and all the people of non-duality. Young's double-slit experiment in quantum mechanics is very useful to explain the non-dual philosophy. One slit is the duality, when the "baby I" (ego) is operating, the world appears real and as matter. If and when, one can drop the ego and perceive from the other slit - that is, non-duality - it appears as one unified spirit or energy or consciousness.

Sri Ramesh Balsekar says you are not the one who cast the spell of ignorance. Hence you cannot remove it. The author's perspective is that the requirements of a spiritual aspirant are a keen urge to know the Truth, gain correct knowledge, dispassion, and self-restraint. Whether you attain the Oneness or not, proper knowledge, understanding, and some spiritual practice will make you a better individual for sure. Even if we do not wake up to the Reality, we can try to make the dream a better one. And you will be changing the script for the better in the hyperloop of the *Karma* concept.

In the beginning, the author mentioned individual consciousness merging with universal consciousness. It was never separate; just an apparent separation. You are not what you "think" you are, my dear reader; you are the untainted "I am". But so is everyone. Don't think you alone are That! You are That. The author is That. Everyone and everything are That. That alone exists. That is the ultimate knowledge.

SIGNIFICANCE OF *GURU*

For some reason, spirituality has flourished and continues to flourish in India. (That doesn't mean spirituality belongs to India). Consequently, there are a plethora of spiritual sects and *gurus* in India. Serious spiritual seekers from across the globe come to India in search of the Truth. In the wide spectrum, it is sometimes difficult to know where and whom to turn to.

In *Sanatana Dharma* traditions, a lot of importance is given to the *Guru*, who is considered equivalent to the Hindu trinity of gods – Brahma, Vishnu, and Maheshwara. This is because a true *Guru* is the one who has extensive knowledge of the scriptures, experience of different practices, has transcended the duality, knows the metaphysics inside out and can give the disciple the knowledge and help the disciple transcend the duality. This repeats through the Teacher-disciple chain, called "*Guru-Sishya parampara*".

Each of these lineages is based in an *Ashram* or *Mutt* and have a particular system of spirituality, based on a particular place, deity, scripture, or a method and adhere to it diligently. For one to be included in the fold, one needs to be in the *Ashram*, initiated and follow the rules of the place, learn, practice and become an adept like the *Guru*. These are closed groups and are not for casual or part-time seekers. It is a dedicated and long commitment.

All religions have this system in place. Traditionally people trained in one of these places come out and guide the public in spirituality-related matters, which usually takes the form of prayers and rituals in the local places of worship. This, as you know, forms the major chunk of spirituality-related matters and what most people think of as religion and their connection to God. In the analogy of Delhi bloggers, not all of these preachers may have reached Delhi; but they have a fair knowledge of the subject and can direct people in the direction of Delhi.

Some people like the author, do not have the time to spend full-time in an *ashram*; at the same time the local place of worship is not enough for their spiritual quest. This brings us to the next group of spiritual teachers who give us some knowledge and some form of practice (*Sadhana*). There are a number of such groups that have proliferated in the past few decades. With this wide array of spiritual houses, it is difficult to know who to turn to. Even the local preacher knows more than an average person. Learn from the local preacher or the modern spiritual houses as much as you can. For an illiterate, elementary school teacher must teach the alphabet. The elementary school teacher may continue to be an elementary school teacher. The student may go on to learn much more than the teacher. Likewise, in spirituality also, learn from all the teachers and teachings. But aim for the PhD, reaching "Delhi" in our analogy.

The modern spiritual houses are like factories. You follow the set pattern and get whatever benefit you get out of it. If that is enough for you, carry on. If you want to go further in spirituality, you must do a lot of self-study with an open mind. Read different scriptures by different authors. As mentioned before, the teachings come in a cryptic way and you need a good interpreter.

True *Gurus* don't solicit students; they are not on the billboards. For them, there is no "You and I". For them, all are one. They simply try to guide those who come to them. For a truly enlightened master, there is no difference between the most ardent student and the most vicious critic. No difference between the roadside beggar and the patron of the *ashram*. A teacher who has truly transcended will see no difference between himself/herself and the rest of the creation. Such a person is the equivalent of God. If you find such a *Guru*, surrender. Faith is of utmost importance in the spiritual path, but do not repose your faith blindly.

There is a plethora of books from such realized masters; written by themselves or usually by their followers. Try to read those and give more importance to the teachings of such masters. The hallmark of a true master is that they do not have any ego or personal agenda whatsoever. Plenty of information is available on the net and across the social media platforms. Within this framework, learn and practice how best you can. Give due importance and respect to your immediate teacher but do not idolize them and make them gods.

It is very important to have self-discipline, self-restraint, and to develop virtues. Most of the masters advise military discipline. Sri Jiddu Krishnamurti says it should not be like that. If you force discipline on your mind, it will rebel. Better to understand the reason and then wilfully develop virtues. Either way, leading a virtuous life is important. Food cravings & carnal instincts (especially for men) are difficult to overcome. Virtue is not just in outward action and appearances. It should be in the thoughts also. It is important to keep a watch on how your thought process and behavior is, even when you are not sitting in meditation.

Knowledge, especially half-baked, with no devotion or love, is dangerous. Likewise, devotion without proper knowledge or love is dangerous and leads to blind faith. Do not make any *guru* god. Once the ego is dissolved completely, there is no you, no god, or *guru*. All is one. When all is one, you can neither be a disciple nor a *guru*. But some *guru* is required to show you the path. Give due importance to your *guru* (seniors) and try to show the correct path to other seekers (juniors). It is the knowledge that is to be revered as god, not the physical form of the teacher. Don't get into the feeling that my *guru* is god and later, the fancy that I am god to my students. Once the self-realization happens completely, there is only Oneness.

As you explore the spiritual literature and scriptures, you will find many things and pearls of wisdom. However, the best of all is within you, within all of us. As Swami Sivananda put succinctly, the best *Guru* is within. It so happens, the biggest obstacle is within too. It is up to oneself to use the wisdom and the tools provided by the seers to shed various layers of ignorance and discover the light within. The correct spiritual journey is always inward and unique to each individual. One can take pointers from seniors in the process and take course correction measures as and when necessary.

The author's experience is that the correct knowledge and path opens up when the time is ripe and one's quest is earnest. The teaching may come in the form of a person, book, video, or a life incident. You must be receptive to understand. The essence of higher spirituality is to go beyond the names and forms. Listen to your inner voice. Be honest with yourself. No need to prove anything to anyone in the spiritual journey. It is purely personal. You may share with like-minded people about the practices and experiences, so that you may help one another.

"One needs to have an intelligent mind, a loving heart, and a selfless-serving attitude. If nothing else, then a realized Master as *Guru*. If not with a realized *Guru*, one must at least be immersed in the books of such realised *Gurus*, before venturing into any modern practices"- Sri Siddharth T Janakiraman on Quora.

FOOD AND HEALTH

Anything in spirituality cannot go without a mention of food and health. Food is what sustains us. Unless one is in good physical health, one cannot think or progress in the spiritual path. The food that we consume affects our physical health. The simplest example is, if you consume too hot a thing, it will burn the insides. Most things are not so obvious as the human body is very resilient and has remarkable capacity of healing itself. Due to this, people are not able to observe the link between their food and their health.

The craving to please the tongue is there all the time. There is convenience of various types of ready-made and fast foods. Here again the industry (food processing and manufacturing) is mostly misleading the public. Together, these are leading most people to abuse their bodies in all possible ways and inviting ill health. Things to avoid are all types of meat; if possible, all animal products. Processed suger is one of the worst things for our health. One rule of thumb is to consume locally produced food, processed as little as possible.

Avoid or minimize all types of intoxicants like alcohol and cigarettes. Things you consume should not be too hot or too cold. Avoid white sugar as much as possible. You need not become a saint all at once! Just understand the principles and try to bring in whatever and however much change you want to bring into your life. You can cheat once in a while! Never consume anything in fear; if you are not sure, avoid it.

Do not drag yourself into guilt or fear either because of eating something or not eating something. Whatever you are eating, eat in peaceful surroundings without disturbances and with reverence for food. Spare a thought and thank everyone who helped in bringing that food onto your plate. If you want to know more about food and how the food industry and scientists can mislead us knowingly or unknowingly, please read The Chinese Study. Also read *Ikigai*, the Japanese way.

There is an enormous amount of misery and suffering in society, most of it untold or sometimes in disguise. As a doctor, the author gets to see a lot of patients whose underlying cause of the illness is some form of fear, anxiety, or a lack of proper food. These manifest as various physical ailments including psychosomatic disorders. The emphasis in the present healthcare system is to treat the manifestations only. Nobody bothers to look into the underlying reasons and rectify them, let alone prevent them. You must develop awareness and take care of your food and thereby your health.

CONSUMERISM

Sri Yuval Noah Harari in his book Sapiens explains the agricultural revolution and mentions how domesticating and growing maize has changed our hunter-gatherer forefathers into settlers, who then formed societies. He muses: Is it humans that domesticated the maize, or maize that domesticated humans? We must apply this to our current situation: Is it humans using science and technology, or the other way around? Have we become slaves of technology?

Please do not misunderstand. The author is not against science and technology; without them, it would not be possible to write this and communicate with you so easily. It is about overuse of comforts and technology. It is an individual choice. Use the modern-day comforts and technology sensibly and consciously. Do not be a slave to technology. The more you crave and cling to these various material comforts, the more mental restlessness, fear, and anxiety you will have.

There has been a tremendous increase in the usage of chemicals. Please look around you. Just to give a few examples: at home we use toothpaste, soap, washing powder, toilet cleaner, perfumes, deodorants, cigarettes, alcohol. A lot more chemicals go into manufacturing, construction, farming and animal husbandry. Almost all medicines are chemicals. Many chemicals increase the risk of cancer. We cannot boycott the chemicals. We simply cannot do it. Our lives are so dependent on many of these chemicals. Use them judiciously and avoid those that can be avoided.

The human psyche wants new experiences. Starting from the toothpaste/soap to clothes to cell phone to movie-going experience to holidays, it wants novelty. It craves variety and wants more. It is a natural tendency. It fuels innovation and growth. Of late, due to technological advances, the change has become exponential. We are seeing rapid introduction of products. The turnover time for new products has reduced considerably. This has created a problem in the collective psyche of people. They want more, industry is providing more, it is being gobbled and they want even more. This is good for the economy and industrial growth. At the individual level, if people are not careful and mindful, they become zombies in the system. Their brain is taken over by what is happening in society and are running mindlessly. By the time they realize that their appetite for material goods and experiences is insatiable, life is over. It is important to sit back and reflect upon things every now and then. Stabilize your mind, steer your life in the direction that you want, with the speed you are comfortable with; rather than the speed set by the society and industry.

Take a look at your wardrobe. Do you really need all those things that you have been storing? Next time you go for shopping, pause and think whether you really need to buy new clothes. Don't buy the latest gadget (cell phone, cars, etc.) that is released just for the sake of it or because your friend has bought it. Do not host expensive parties and functions beyond your capacity. Take a pause and think whether you really need it or not. Not an easy thing to get over the cravings. Again, if you make a conscious effort, they will slowly fade away. The usual response is: How can one live without medicines and clothes? You cannot, but use them wisely, try to understand the word "Thrift".

Thrift is not good for the economy. That is another thing: Has the economic growth overtaken the individual's health and welfare? People living virtuously and with thrift are not good for the economy. Someone who eats only vegetarian food, does not smoke or consume alcohol, walks or cycles to work, eats out very little, exercises regularly and tries to stay healthy is not at all good for the economy. The industry wants you to do exactly the opposite. It is in your own interest not to fall prey to consumerism.

Do you want to lead an automated life prescribed by the society, family, friends or take things into your hands and change your lifestyle for the better? It is up to you. It is an individual choice where to draw the line. It need not be an all-or-none thing. You decide how much change you want to bring into your life. We need not rewind the clock and be like our "hunter-gatherer" forefathers. It is not possible for any of us to do that. Just bring some awareness into your thought process and make choices in life. To quote Lord Buddha: take the "middle path". Spirituality encompasses all our activities, including how we live. Try to live sensibly and leave as small a carbon footprint as you can on mother earth for your sake, our sake and the future generations' sake.

For youngsters: the only basic thing that a human needs is food. Everything else is an add-on. That doesn't mean one should simply eat and be content. There is so much life has to offer. Don't be lazy. Try to get as much knowledge as possible; both in your chosen field and other fields. Work hard. Lead your life sensibly. Do not get addicted to anything; alcohol, sex, work, exercise, knowledge, charity, power, popularity. Anything in excess is not good. Do not get hooked on the reflected glory of your cricket/football clubs/players or movie actors. Try to develop and express your own creativity through music, poetry and painting. Balance all aspects of your life. Always try to give more than you take in any relationship, including nature. Never be greedy. Never let failures drag you down. Learn from the mistakes and move on. Life doesn't stop for anyone. It is a continuum. Do not get stuck in any situation, good or bad. Everything will eventually pass. All relationships will end one day. Do not get dependent on any relationship, personal, business, or job. Cherish, protect and enjoy the relationships as long as they last. When you have done your part to the family and society, turn to spirituality.

BEING HUMAN

Being human is a double-edged sword. We are far better, miles apart from our fellow animals. That puts enormous responsibility on us. They do not have the intellect and live an automated life in tune with nature. Humans, on the other hand, have the intellect and discriminatory power and can choose. A good number of people, however, are living an automated life, pursuing some passion or the other, destroying mother earth in the pursuit of ever-transitory happiness through "I want more" or "I want a new experience". Look at Maslow's pyramid. People who are at the base of the pyramid are not much different from our fellow animals. We must use our intellect and try to reach the higher levels of evolution.

If you "try" to be happy based on the external circumstances, happiness will be short-lived. It always follows a phase of emptiness and wanting more. If you get rid of all the conditioning and still the mind, joy wells up in you, without any reason.

The greed of the mind propels us towards material comforts and the ever-elusive happiness. Many people seem to be happy outwardly in society. If you see them close enough, they are full of negative emotions: fear, jealousy, hatred, resentment, etc. True happiness is not having any of the negative emotions. It can be achieved only when the mind is tamed and the oscillations of the mind are switched off, so to speak.

You have two choices: one is to believe in what you see in the observable universe and think that there is nothing more to life than an accumulation of atoms governed by selfish genes. There is no purpose to this life. It is just by accident that you happened to be here. The other view is that your life has a purpose. There is a reason, based on the law of causality, that each and every one of us is present on Earth. Try to find out who you really are and what your purpose is on Earth.

The core restlessness makes us cling to different things for support, like family, religion, nation, or some social group based on some common interests, etc. We create labels based on these associations and find security in them. This in turn causes polarization: mine vs. not mine. This polarization is the root cause of conflict in society. It doesn't allow us to be neutral in our thought process. If someone has done something wrong, we judge it based on the various labels attached to ourselves and to the culprit. If the culprit belongs to "our" group, we take a lenient view. Otherwise, we are more aggressive in seeking redress. Starting from a minor traffic violation to major policy decisions that can alter the course of the nation, we have the same partisanship. We are making anything into a "tug of war" by taking sides, based on our ideology or labels. We do not judge the matter at hand based on its merits or demerits and make a decision in an impartial way. This leads to resentment in the other group and escalates the conflict. The perpetual cycle of hatred and wars continue.

There is only one person you can change in the entire universe – yourself. If you try to reduce the conflict in your mind, and be more balanced, it will automatically reduce the conflict in society and make it a better place for all of us to live and for the future generations. Most of the conflicts either within or without are due to generations-old concepts, misapprehensions, misinformation, dogma, fear, trying to prove superiority over one another and polarization based on one's beliefs and labels. Author's appeal is for people to understand the commonality in our lives, views, and to try to reduce the self-centredness a little bit and reduce the conflict at individual, societal, and national level. It must start at an individual level.

It is God's (or natural selection, whatever word you want to use) wish and design that we explore, enjoy and express ourselves in all possible ways. God is sort of expressing and exploring itself. However, if you follow your biological instincts and carry on, you are simply living an automated life that depends on the effects of nature, planets and people around you. This usually leaves a considerable amount of dissatisfaction, some emptiness and feeling of lack in the end. One wants to fulfil that void by doing various unnecessary things. People are turning everything into an industry and religion. In our collective ignorance we are falling prey to so many unnecessary things. One must start looking inwards. The author does not prescribe this to youngsters. They must explore life. Unless one does things in material life, one cannot or perhaps should not turn to spirituality. Only advice to them is not to abuse their bodies and minds too much with various substances or ideologies. Not to indulge too much in sensual pleasures and for too long. They can still follow some of the things mentioned in Consumerism and Simple rules. Once you get over the age of 50, or at least by 60 you must turn to spirituality in earnest.

We come across many people who are well-to-do in life in many aspects but mired in misery due to lack of something or other. It is a general tendency for the mind to take for granted whatever we have achieved. However much you have achieved in the form of money, status, education, fame, sarees, jewellery, anything – it wants more or some other thing. There is always a gap between reality and expectation.

This gap is actually what propels us to improve ourselves. If we were happy with the telephone, we would not have got the cellular phone and later the smartphone. If you are too content, you will not progress in life. If you always want more, you will never be happy in life. Try to understand the expectation-reality mismatch and work your life around it. Always be thankful to God/

Life for whatever you "have" in life. Try to improve or get "more", but do not be too greedy.

If you wake up in the morning in reasonably good physical health, that itself is a great blessing. Start your day with a "Thank God for Everything". Try to give whatever you can give to less privileged people. Giving doesn't necessarily have to be money. It need not be to poor people. It can be that also. It can be lending a helping hand to a friend, listening to someone going through a rough patch, teaching a skill to someone; it can be any act of random kindness. Even giving way to a pedestrian while going in a car is giving. Thank God that you are in a position to give. See how the "joy of giving" takes you to a different plane altogether. One catch is: you must give without expecting anything in return. If you expect anything back, you will fall into the trap of "expectation-reality" mismatch!

Never advertise or brag about your charitable acts. We see a lot of it these days. For someone on the spiritual path, it is a big no, as it feeds and strengthens your ego. You must understand that there is "selfishness" in charity. On the surface it looks as if you are giving, but you get something out of it – name, fame or just the "feel-good factor". Some people may find it difficult to understand what the author calls concept B. Concept A is the receiver thanking the giver. Concept B is the giver thanking the receiver. If you look closely, the idea is to tame the "ego". Concept A tends to pamper the giver's ego; whereas concept B makes one humble and reduces the ego.

The author wants all of you to consider this in the "giver-receiver" transactions in life. Try to give whatever you can give, without expecting anything in return. Be thankful to the Almighty, who gave you the power or resources to give and to the receiver for accepting whatever you are offering. Keep concept B in mind and see how it will transform your life.

Do not get into the trap. Give wholeheartedly without expecting anything, not even a thank you from the receiver. You will then truly get into the "Joy of giving". Nothing you give with good intention will ever be wasted. You will see the universe reciprocating you in many ways, mifold.

Whether you agree with the information and logic in this book or not, do any spiritual practices or not after reading this book, just try to bring in a little bit of awareness into your life. Try to be a good human being. Take care of your body by taking healthy food, doing some exercise and avoiding intoxicants. Help others in your own way, and most importantly avoid the partisan attitude.

SIMPLE RULES

Follow the religion of your choice, with faith and devotion. Not with fear of retribution and compulsion. If you follow the basic tenets of any religion by following self-restraint, respecting all life forms and nature, you are on the correct path.

Do not fight in the name of religion and God. God is one. God does not need your help to prove his strength. If you are fighting or spreading hatred in the name of God, you are simply distancing yourself from God. Spirituality must be silent. It is your inner journey to discover who you are.

Develop awareness in all that you do. Be a witness to your activities and thoughts. Do not be judgmental of anyone or any situation. Analyze impartially. Follow AUM – be Aware, Understand and do Mindful action. It is easy to remember and is also the primordial sound, which transformed to Om, Amen, Ameen.

Practice some form of *yoga* and/or meditation. Keep judging yourself whether you are progressing and noticing improvement in yourself. Do not get entangled in the names and symbols.

Do not expect results overnight! It is a slow process. If you keep up the practice, you will notice the changes over a period of time. Milestones to look for are losing the negative emotions: fear, anxiety, anger, envy etc., and a rise in the positive emotions.

At some point in time you may have to choose between continuing in or renouncing the material world. The author suggests continuing in the material world with "mental renunciation". Do not indulge in material comforts blindly. Use them sensibly.

Be aware of what you are eating and drinking. Plant-based food which is fresh, wholesome and not processed too much is good. Eat with reverence for food and not in a hurry. Remember, food is for sustenance; not for indulgence.

Try to do some form of fasting, provided your health permits, to overcome the physical dependence on food. Try Lord Buddha's "noble silence" as propounded by Sri Goenka, where you are in solitude and stay off all forms of communication. This will help reduce the psychological dependence on people, gadgets and the external world as such.

Spend at least 30 minutes a day in meditation, contemplation, or introspection. The simplest way is Sri

Ramana's: Sit comfortably in a quiet place, focus on the heart and contemplate "I am".

There are several *Gurus* and ways out there. Follow anyone that suits your taste. But do not get entangled in the means and ways! Your aim is to become as enlightened as the *Guru*, not to idolize him/her. Do not get lost in the process.

Worship the energy or consciousness that is the undercurrent of the cosmos. It vibrates across the universe in all things in the universe including you. It is the driving force behind everything seen and unseen. If you can turn inwards and touch that dimension, you will be complete. The search, the feeling of lack, ends. All the masters concur that it is the ultimate or perhaps only goal of being born as a human.

Taking the spiritual pursuit with proper understanding and guidance will remove all the fear and forbearance. Enjoy the remaining part of your life and you may even get enlightened in the bargain!

EPILOGUE

Let us look at the commonality that the author mentioned at the beginning of this book. The commonality in religions is that: 1. There is a transcendental phenomenon that is beyond the normal sensory perception we call God. 2. There are some people who have experienced that dimension using different means and shared their knowledge with common people. 3. People who had that knowledge or their followers set up places of worship and tried to propagate that knowledge through various means. 4. They set up rules to live in a society in a harmonious way and also gave information on how to experience that metaphysical phenomenon. 5. They warned that if one doesn't follow the rules set by them, common people will be punished by God.

From this basic core theme, the rest of the proliferation happened. If you look at the bare bones of any religion, this remains the essence. One important point in serious spirituality is that you must know how much importance to give to names and forms. You need the names and forms to live in society and get the knowledge, but do not get entangled in them. You must transcend them if you want to experience the meta-physical phenomenon. Secondly, one must understand that the "fear of God" is inculcated to keep the society in order. One must be "God-fearing" with proper understanding and lead a virtuous life. This should not be made into a negative thing to get blackmailed. The actual mechanism is *Karma*, by which one reaps the results of one's actions. Every action of yours will come back to you sooner or later.

A good amount of the information in this book is not new. The author's interpretation of some of the things and the thoughts that came out are not the author's own. They just passed through the mind while in contemplation. As Sri Nisargadatta mentioned, those sorts of thoughts come from the other dimension. Perhaps that is the reason why ancient *Rishis* never claimed ownership of the Vedas and left them as "*Apaurusheyas*"; meaning, not created by humans.

You may get some extra power or intuition (*Siddhis*) along the way. Do not get entangled in such things. If you start exhibiting them, you will go off the course. It is just tricks of the "baby I" to mislead you. Don't get attracted to someone who is exhibiting any such powers. As often repeated, you have everything in you, you just need to change your perspective.

Try to look into the innermost core of your being. Some people may not be able to do it on their own. Take the help of a *guru* if you want. But most of them have their own inadequacies and may not lead you to the Ultimate. In a perfect *Guru*, you will not see any trace of selfishness or selfish motives. A perfect example is Sri Ramana. Next best is someone who can point you in the correct direction, even if they are not enlightened or perfect themselves. All the knowledge is out there and within. You just have to keep looking. If your seeking is ardent, the information will come to you automatically. (Ask, and it will be given to you; seek, and you will find; knock, and the door will be opened to you. Matthew 7:7.) It may come in the form of a person, an incident, social media post/video or a book. You just have to be aware and receptive.

As can be seen from the list of references, the author has tried a variety of things, but there appeared some flaw, some limitation, some blockage: either in the teacher or the teachings or the methods. The quest continued. One after the other, different layers of ignorance were transcended. Finally, with the teachings of Sri Ramana Maharshi and Sri Nisargadatta Maharaj, the final pieces in the jigsaw puzzle fell into place, as far as the theoretical aspect is concerned. Further help came in the form of Satsang from his medical school classmates headed by Dr. Srinivasa Reddy and Sri Yellamraju Srinivasa Rao's exposition on Sri Sankara *Advaita* (www.advaitavedanta.in).

Spiritual path is not easy. It is arduous, especially in the initial stages. You need guidance. People around you may not understand. You may get frustrated. But it is worth it. You may go through a phase of negative emotions, popularly known as the "dark night of the soul". If you feel that way, seek appropriate help.

All are saying the same thing in different languages and styles. Anyone who is enlightened must say the same thing. Because Truth is one. Just like the mountaineers using different equipment and paths to reach the top, different religions and *Gurus* are passing on their paths and equipment to their disciples. As it is a sacred path, it comes with vows to respect the teacher and the path. One formula doesn't suit all. Everyone is different. Work your way around in the maze. The culmination is Oneness or *Advaita* or non-duality.

Pure *Advaita* may sound like Buddhism or even atheism, but it is not. It encompasses everything that is manifest and unmanifest. In the non-dual realm, only the supreme knowledge remains. Both the knower and the known are merged back into the knowledge. All names, forms (including those of gods and *gurus*) and even scriptures are negated. But you will see that even *Advaitins* are hooked onto names and forms of Sri Sankara or someone else. The names and forms are necessary to understand and shift the perception to perceive the Formless. Due respect should be given, but there should be no bondage.

We tend to waste time most of the day, with the mind going back and forth. Try to avoid that by: reading books – *Jnana*; contemplation on God – *Bhakti*; doing some good work – *Karma*. These are different ways of keeping the mind occupied and taking control of it. Do not blame anyone or any situation. Just try to better it. If you cannot change it, remind yourself that this too will pass, nothing is permanent. Do not keep arguing about how to overcome social injustice. If you can do something about the social injustice, do. You may notice some changes in the way things happen. Maybe chance happenings. It looks as if the universe is conspiring in your favour.

Do not get blinded by dogmas - religious, political, or intellectual. Try to see through the veil of ignorance and the commonality that we all share. The mind is there to keep up the divisiveness. It is designed that way. It is not possible to stay in the non-dual realm all the time. Baby I wants to continue clinging to the various identities and conditionings. You must carry on the day-to-day conduct of life as usual depending on the social circumstances and society's norms where you live.

While carrying on the external activities as usual, keep looking inwards and develop awareness. As you progress, you will not jump to conclusions about any situation or incident based on your preset mind. You will analyse it and come to a conclusion based on the merits and demerits. You would not like to take sides, which may be a problem as people around you identifying themselves with labels would like you to join the tug-of-war. You must analyse every situation freshly and take a decision which you feel is appropriate. If more people follow this method, there will be less partisanship in the society and the conflicts will come down.

A little bit of bondage is necessary for survival. It is a fundamental and inherent part of nature. We have to breathe, eat, work, and socialize to some extent. Bondage should not lead to misery. No need to renounce anything. Renounce mentally. What is yours to renounce anyway? It is all a mental game. What you must lose is the "attachment" to various things and identification with body and mind. Then you are liberated. In case you happen to be liberated, author's request is not to start yet another spiritual group or path; there are too many already. Do not add to the confusion!

Spirituality is the core of our existence; it forms the basis of all religions and subsects and all the modern spiritual houses. The acid test of spiritual maturity is that it should make you a better individual. You must be at peace with yourself and the people around you. Otherwise, you are on the wrong track. Hope this information helps you and society in some way. Even a little change will slowly get bigger. Thank you so much for reading. May you and all beings be happy and peaceful. Love to all.

REFERENCES

The author has tried to read varied scriptures: Bhagavad Gita, Holy Bible, and Holy Quran. The following books have helped the author immensely in the spiritual quest. The author suggests reading the first three books at a later stage as these are heavily non-dual and may not be comprehensible to an average mind.

Be As You Are, Teachings of Sri Ramana Maharshi, David Godman, Penguin Random House 1992.

A Search In Secret India, Paul Brunton, Random House 2003.

I am That: Talks with Sri Nisargadatta Maharaj, Sudhakar S. Dikshit, Chetana Private 2003.

The Gospel of Sri Ramakrishna – Abridged Edition, Mr M, Swami Nikhilananda, Sri Ramakrishna Math.

The Vedas, Sri Chandrasekharendra Saraswati, Bharatiya Vidya Bhavan 2016.

Autobiography of a Yogi, Paramahansa Yogananda, Yogoda Satsang Society of India 2005.

The Power of Now, Eckhart Tolle, Namaste Publishing 2004.

Watching Your Life, Teja Anand, Anatta Press 2019.

Awareness - The Key to Living in Balance, Osho, St. Martin's Griffin 2001.

Secrets of Karma, Vee Jay Attri, Trinity 2016.

The Problems of Spiritual Life, Swami Krishnananda, The Divine Life Society.

May I Answer That, Swami Sivananda, The Divine Life Society.

Amrita Gita, Swami Sivananda, The Divine Life Society.
Drg Drsya Viveka, Swami Nikhilananda, Advaita Ashrama 2019.
Consciousness Speaks, Ramesh S Balsekar, Zen Publications 2011.
Your Head In Tiger's Mouth, Ramesh S Balsekar, Zen Publications 2011.
Inner Engineering - A Yogi's Guide to Joy, Sadhguru, Penguin Ananda, 2016.
The Dharmapada, Eknath Easwaran, Jaico, 2012.
The Long Road Turns to Joy, Thich Nhat Hanh, Parallax Press, 2011.
You are the World, J Krishnamurti, Krishnamurti Foundation India 2010.
The First and Last Freedom, J Krishnamurti, Rider 2013.
If Truth Be Told - A Monk's Memoir, Om Swami, Harper Element 2014.
Mind Full to Mindful, Om Swami, Harper Collins 2018.
The Ancient Science of Mantras, Om Swami, Jaico 2020.
The Hidden Power of Gayatri Mantra, Om Swami, Jaico 2019.
The Vision of Karma Yoga, Swami Tattvavidananda Saraswati, Brahma Vidya Kuteer 2018.
Kaupeena Panchakam, Swami Tattvavidananda Saraswati, Brahma Vidya Kuteer 2018.
Manasa Bodha, Swami Vidyaprakasananda Giri, Sri Sukabrahmasramam 2023.
MetaHuman, Deepak Chopra, Penguin Random House 2019.

A Brief History of Time, Stephen Hawking, Bantam Books 1995.
The Grand Design, Stephen Hawking, Bantam Books 2011.
Brief Answers to Big Questions, Stephen Hawking, John Murray Publishers 2018.
The Selfish Gene, Richard Dawkins, Oxford University Press 2006.
Sapiens - A Brief History of Humankind, Yuval Nova Harari, Vintage 2011.
Homo Deus: A Brief History of Tomorrow, Yuval Nova Harari Vintage 2016.

Dark Matter and Dark Energy, Brian Clegg, Icon Books 2019.
The Book of Woman, Osho, Penguin Ananda 2013.
The Book of Man, Osho, Penguin Ananda 2013.
Shunya - A Novel, Sri M, Westland Publications Pvt Ltd 2018.
Decoding Karma, Michael CJ Fox, Amazon 2019.

Illusions: The Adventures of a Reluctant Messiah, Richard Bach, Dell 1977.
The Alchemist, Paulo Coelho, Harper Torch 1988.
The Monk Who Sold His Ferrari, Robin Sharma, Harper 1999.
The Secret, Rhonda Byrne, Atria Books 2006.
Believing is Seeing, Michael Guillen, Tyndale 2021.
Feeling is the Secret, Neville Goddard, Sanage Publishing House LLP 2021.
The China Study, T. Colin Campbell, Thomas M Campbell, Ben Bella Books 2016.
Ikigai: The Japanese secret to a long and happy life, Hector Garcia, Francesc Miralles, Cornerstone 2017.

In addition, the author is helped by various "Seniors" who have trodden the path:

Swami Tattvavidananda Saraswati: Personal interaction and guidance.
Swamī Parākāsthānanda: Personal interaction and guidance.
Dr Pandu Yenumula: Personal interaction and sharing experiences.
Dr Pratap Paruchuru: Upanishad discourses in GEMS Satsang.

Sadhguru Sri Sivananda Murthy: WhatsApp posts from Sivananda Guru Cultural Trust, Warangal.
Sri Satyanarayana Goenka: Vipassana Course, YouTube.
Sadhguru Jaggi Vasudev: Inner Engineering Course, Books, YouTube, WhatsApp.
Sri Sri Ravi Shankar: Sudarshana Kriya, YouTube, WhatsApp.
Sri Krishnaji: Public discourse.
Sri Daaji: Books and visit to Kanha Santivanam.

Siddhartha T Janakiraman, Jay Jennifer Matthews, Teja Anand, David Fox, Brian Jones, Kapil Bhutkar, Rami Sivan and many others on Quora Non-duality spaces.

BK Shivani: YouTube, WhatsApp.
Swami Sarvapriyananda: YouTube.
Swami Mukundanda: YouTube.
Sri Dandapani: YouTube.
Mr. Leo (Actualized.org): YouTube.
Supreme Yogi Channel: YouTube.
Sai Satsangh Columbia (saiarathi.blogspot.com): Personal Communication
Sri Mahatria: WhatsApp.
PKConsciousness: WhatsApp.
https://greenmesg.org
(translation for sloka on the last page)

ॐ सर्वेशां स्वस्तिर्भवतु ।
सर्वेशां शान्तिर्भवतु ।
सर्वेशां पुर्णंभवतु ।
सर्वेशां मङ्गलंभवतु ।
ॐ शान्तिः शान्तिः शान्तिः ॥

Om Sarveshaam Svastir-Bhavatu |
Sarveshaam Shaantir-Bhavatu |
Sarveshaam Purnam-Bhavatu |
Sarveshaam Mangalam-Bhavatu |
Om Shaantih Shaantih Shaantih ||

Meaning:
May there be Well-Being in All
May there be Peace in All
May there be Fulfilment in All
May there be Auspiciousness in All
Om Peace, Peace, Peace